ANGELS IN HEAVEN AND EARTH

by

Stephen D. Swihart

Logos International
Plainfield, New Jersey

All Scripture references are taken from the New International Version of the Bible unless otherwise noted as KJV, King James Version.

Preface

References to God's angels appear over 375 times in the Bible. Their appearance may be found in thirty-four of the Bible's sixty-six books (in 44 percent of the Old Testament books and in 67 percent of the New Testament books).

The devil, along with his companion fallen angels and demons, are mentioned over 300 times in the Bible. In the Gospels alone we read of these evil forces at least 116 times, more frequently than we see the words "love," "gospel," "peace," "repent," or "Spirit." Another seventy references to the devil can be found in the rest of the New Testament, from the book of Acts through the book of the Revelation. Of the twenty-seven New Testament books only four do not have references to Satanology.

This abundance of revelation on the subject demands recognition. There can be no full or accurate understanding of God's dealings with people if we should for some reason bypass or treat lightly this topic of Scripture.

If you want facts (and not fantasies) about angels, you must read God's Word. He created them, gives them their orders and carefully monitors their every activity. Current numerous reported appearances of angels have raised a high degree of interest in their nature and doings. But some, if not much, of this kind of information has caused a certain uneasiness among varying Christian circles.

There is no intent in this writing to be critical of angelic reality or the involvement of angels in the affairs of this world. But an alarm is set off when current, popular statements are made regarding angelic visitations that do not conform to the written and infallible record of the Scriptures. Much extrabiblical data concerning angels is being circulated; such information has no biblical basis.

The attempt here is to present the scriptural teaching regarding angels. The content is deliberately concise, but at the same time I've also tried to be precise and thorough. It is with the mood of joy and for the purpose of corrective edification (or possible protective edification) that this labor is offered to the Body of Christ.

Contents

CONTENTS

ANGELS
IN HEAVEN
AND EARTH

PART I

GOOD ANGELS

1

A Historical Overview of Angels

The doctrine of angels is not restricted to the Scriptures. Unfortunately, there is quite a bit of misinformation about angels to be found outside of the Bible. It is this added material that has contributed so abundantly to our current confusion. Let's examine some of the general data that claims to be Christian, but, in the end, proves to be false.

Syncretistic Threats

The word "syncretism" may be unfamiliar to you, so here is its meaning: "the combination of various beliefs or practices which results in new beliefs or practices." Often liberal theologians envision much of the biblical teachings as being

3

only the fusion of the ideas that were present in surrounding cultures. Obviously, this denies the inspiration of the Scriptures and ought to be soundly rejected by all Christians. Still, the threat of syncretism exists today.

There were many doctrines about angels in the ancient world. Angels were acknowledged by the Persians, Babylonians, Chaldeans, Greeks and many others. Liberal students see in the Scriptures a conglomeration of these pagan ideas. Conservative scholarship, however, dismisses this notion in favor of biblical inspiration.

Because of the fact that not everyone is conservative in their theology, there is to this day a strong interest in ghosts, goblins, reincarnation, seances and the like. Each of these beliefs rises from pagan cultures and their false gods. Regrettably, many who subscribe to these ideas (and other similar beliefs) do so while supposedly retaining a devotion to the Bible. This practice is called syncretism. It has been with us since the beginning, and it won't disappear before Christ returns.

There is a great deal of material on angels outside of the Bible—more outside than inside! Gustav Davidson, probably the foremost authority on these extrabiblical angels, has actually written a nearly 400-page dictionary on this theme alone (*A Dictionary of Angels: Including the Fallen Angels*, The Free Press, New York,

Collier-MacMillan, 1967).

Page after page of material on angels can be found in the pseudepigrapha (a large collection of Jewish writings not found in the biblical canon—written between B.C. 200 and A.D. 200), the Talmud (Jewish interpretations of the Old Testament—written by A.D. 500), Gnostic literature (a Christian-type cult of the first centuries after Christ), patristic writings (the works of the early church leaders), the Koran (the bible of the Moslems), folklore, black magic manuals, ancient church statements, and other related writings.

We are tempted to ask how did these extrabiblical writers come up with such diverse and intricate stories of angels. Davidson believes that the majority of these episodes have come as a result of mystical concentration. While Davidson accepts this ascetic devotion to the spirit world, the Bible is swift to renounce the vast bulk of these experiences as coming from Satan (see Gal. 1:6-10; 1 Tim. 4:1-3; 2 Tim. 4:2-5; etc.).

Angels in Art

Oftentimes theology is conveyed through art. What people are taught and what they believe is often expressed through an artist's brush. Such is the case with angels.

In the first 300 years of the early Church the artistic depictions of angels were aligned with biblical descriptions. They were drawn to appear as men. By the end of the 300's, however, Church officials began to take special notice of these angelic beings, almost worshiping them. Some Church historians comment that devotion to the angels became so intense that entire cults developed around them—especially around Michael and Gabriel.

Michael was the first angel to have his own cult. The development of legends around this angelic messenger soon spawned unique devotion to him. Constantine the Great (c. A.D. 280-337) even had a church erected in his honor. Later, other churches followed this precedent. Just as the false religions built temples to house their gods, so the church established buildings for dead saints and angels. Soon statues of Michael and Gabriel were made and sheltered in these sanctuaries, supposedly to protect the entrance to God's house.

In my research for this writing I came across a book entitled, *Manual of St. Michael the Archangel.* The author explicitly declares that the principal object of the book "is to spread devotion in the hearts of the faithful towards St. Michael the archangel." His book contains 330 pages of material on this single angel! I also found modern prayers that were recommended for use in honoring the angels. There were even formulas offered in some writings on how to conjure up a

6

good angelic spirit!

It was in the late 300's that angels began to appear with wings, staffs in the shape of a cross and/or halos. It wasn't until the 1100's that child-angels showed up in art. This seems to be a carry-over from the classical pagan representation of Cupid, which has remained with us to this very day (as we have many nativity scenes). Child-angels are not, however, a part of Eastern art. This is solely a Western innovation, making little angels cute, sometimes robed, and sometimes naked.

Zoroastrianism (an Eastern religion begun in the fifth century B.C.) is the first religion to introduce females in the angelic host. This faith believes angels can appear in either male or female forms at will. In Babylonian mythology the same picture is presented. Folklore, traditions, reports of female angelic visitations, and art have each served to sustain these unbiblical concepts.

One author says it really doesn't matter that the artists are so diverse in their depiction of the angels; what counts, he says, is the joy we derive from the art itself. False! Art, like every other discipline, should, to the fullest extent of its discernment, reflect the positive posture of the Scriptures. Error in art is as wrong as error in print. Both ought to represent the truth accurately.

In a recently published five-volume Bible dictionary, representing the best in conservative scholarship, there are drawings that depict angels as woman with wings! One wonders if the popular misconception is possible to erase.

Angels in the Academic Arena

Angels have always been a subject of discussion in the Church. Their nature, disposition, rank, names, and service have been written about in each generation since the close of the New Testament canon.

Much of the writing of the early Church leaders conforms to the facts revealed in the Scriptures. Occasionally someone goes beyond the sacred text and adds some novel (though unhelpful) notions. For instance, Clement of Alexandria believed the angels moved the stars; Origen felt they were placed over the four elements: earth, water, air and fire; Hermas taught that angels oversaw all the affairs concerning animals; and Tertullian (along with Clement and Origen) believed that the procreation of babies was impossible without the added assistance of the angels.

It is quite clear that in the first 500 years of the Church there developed a formal cult of angel worship (Col. 2:18). The early Church fathers warned against these groups, calling them idolatrous bodies, and asking for a worship of

God alone, but their efforts seem to have generated little effect.

Within a short while a liturgical feast was given in honor of Michael, the archangel. Masses and prayers in his honor were practiced as early as the 500's.

By the 1300's, theologians were less interested in the veneration of the angels, and more concerned about their nature. Still, there was a strong note of devotion to the angels, especially the archangels. In this period of so-called scholasticism there was yet the continued formation of associations and confraternities in honor of angels. Prayers were often offered to them for protection.

As the centuries have passed, and as the scientific revolution has taken hold of the world with its liberalizing effects, theology about and devotion to the angels has changed very little. Today there can be found as broad a divergence of reactions—from blatant rejection of angels (like that of the Sadducees—Acts 23:8) to devout worship. An example of the latter (devotion to the angels) can be seen in the book entitled *Memoirs of a Guardian Angel*, a 320-page volume which records the story of a particular angel's duties and impressions. In a "Christian" book dated September, 1976, the reader is taught to talk (through prayer) with the angels!

There can be little doubt that there are other

multitudes ready to swallow an angelic story almost at the drop of a hat. This fact is shown no better than in the establishment of the Church of Jesus Christ of Latter-day Saints, or Mormons.

The Latter-day Saints

Probably the most astonishing story that can be found in all the annals of angelic history is the episode that started the Mormon church. According to this cult's records (which, by the way, do not coincide with the historical record), Joseph Smith (in 1820), at the age of fourteen, went into a woods to seek God in prayer. He asked the Lord, "Which of all the sects [denominations] is right?"

In response to this prayer, he reports that two brilliant personages appeared to him. One of the beings then spoke, pointed to the other figure, and said, "This is my beloved Son. Hear Him!"

Three-and-a-half years later after claiming to both see and hear God, the Father and the Son, Joseph Smith reported that he was visited by a heavenly messenger named Moroni. This angelic figure then gave some previously hidden golden plates to him. The plates reportedly contained a detailed account of God's works in the migration of some people from the Tower of Babel to Central America.

Smith related how, along with the plates, special eyeglasses were given to him in order to interpret the Egyptian-type characters. This translation is now called *The Book of Mormon.*

Here comes the punch line: this cult does *not* claim to be a new religion, but instead it asserts itself as being a restoration of the one true Christian faith!

The Mormon church traces its roots to two sources: (1) the written Word of God—the Bible (like yours and mine), and (2) direct revelations from God. These direct revelations are said to continue, either by personal communication from God, or by impressions made upon the mind, or by angels. In the case of the formation of the Mormon church, it was supposedly an angelic being who brought the initial "revelations."

The list of historical errors, scriptural heresies, contradictions and revisions in the writings of Joseph Smith are virtually countless. Yet, the Church of Jesus Christ of Latter-day Saints (Mormons) continues to grow rapidly. Why? Paul explains the cause by saying, *"The spirit [of the ruler of the kingdom of the air, Satan] who is now at work in those who are disobedient"* (Eph. 2:2)!

Let this final warning capture us fully: *"I am astonished that you are so quickly deserting the one who called you by the grace of Christ and are turning to a different gospel—which is really no gospel at all. Evidently some people are throwing you into confusion and are trying to pervert the gospel of Christ. But even if we or an angel from* heaven should preach a gospel other than the one we preached to you, let him be eternally condemned! As we have already said, so now I say again: If anybody is preaching to you a gospel other than what you accepted, let him be eternally condemned!" (Gal. 1:6-9).

2

The Angels Are Created

Their Creation

The angels have not always existed. They were created, like everything else. The Psalmist writes, *"Let them praise the name of the Lord, for he commanded and they were created"* (Ps. 148:5).

In a flash all of the angelic hosts appeared. God commanded their existence, and they were instantly created. When God spoke at the Creation, He said, *"Let there be . . . and it was so"* (see Gen. 1:3, 6, 9, 11, 14-15, 24; etc.). Multiplied millions of years were not necessary in order to create the angels. God merely called them into existence, and they appeared.

The precise time of the angels' creation is stated nowhere. But there is a hint. If we can read

Genesis 1:1 as a chronological account of Creation [*In the beginning God created: 1. the heavens, and 2. the earth*], then it is safe to say that the angels came into reality when all of the heavens were made. This means their creation had to occur sometime prior to the development of the earth.

This idea fits perfectly with Job's account of the earth's creation: "... *I laid the earth's foundation ... while the morning stars sang together and all the angels shouted for joy*" (Job 38: 4, 7).

The popular notion that angels are literal stars and glorified saints has no scriptural basis whatever.

Their Count

How many angelic beings are there? Do we know? The Scriptures are not exact about their number, but they are said to be numerous. Daniel writes, "*Thousands upon thousands attended him [God]; ten thousand times ten thousand [or 100,000,000] stood before him [God]*" (Dan. 7:10). Jesus, on the night of His arrest, told Peter that, if necessary, He could call to His immediate aid "*more than twelve legions of angels*" [or at least 72,000] (Matt. 26:53). The writer of the book of Hebrews states that in the city of the living God, the heavenly Jerusalem, may be found "*thousands upon thousands of angels*" (Heb. 12:22). John states that he saw and heard the voices of countless angels, "*numbering thousands upon thousands, ten thousand times ten thousand*" (Rev. 5:11).

How many angels are there? The biblical writers do not give their actual count. Apparently it isn't important. God has enough angels to accomplish all of His will, and that, in the final analysis, is what really counts!

Their Creator

The Genesis account attributes the angelic creation solely to an act of God. The New Testament gives more detail. Here we read how God used Jesus, the second member of the Godhead, to create angels: "*Through him [the Word—Jesus Christ] all things were made; without him nothing was made that has been made*" (John 1:3). "*For by him [Jesus Christ] all things were created: things in heaven and on earth, visible and invisible, whether thrones or powers or rulers or authorities; all things were created by him and for him*" (Col. 1:16). "*In these last days he [God] has spoken to us by his Son . . . through whom he made the universe*" (Heb. 1:2).

Jesus is far more than the model of a good man with a knack for making profound statements! He is God! The role of Jesus in the creation and establishment of the universe cannot be overlooked. The angels serve *Him*.

Their Cause

The angels are not glorified saints in heaven. Neither are they the last link in some mystical evolutionary chain. No, indeed. Instead, they were created as a separate classification of beings for the purpose of serving Jesus Christ in His management of the universe.

Paul put it plainly and precisely when he said, *"For by him [Jesus Christ] all things were created: things in heaven and on earth . . . all things were created by him and for him"* (Col. 1:16). These last two prepositions hold the key for the cause of the angelic creation—they were made both "by" and "for" Jesus Christ. They belong to Him. He is their Commander-in-Chief. (It should be noted that though God the Father can give angels their orders—Matthew 18:10—there is no clear reference in the Bible to support the current notion of some that it is the Holy Spirit who is in charge of these celestial beings.)

According to secular accounts, the angels were created for a variety of causes. Here is a brief summary: to push the stars around; to oversee the planets; to attend the twenty-eight chambers of the moon; to be the guardian of the months, days, and hours; to act as wardens in the halls of heaven; to rule in the seven heavens; to act as governor of the twelve signs of the Zodiac; to oversee the four seasons, and so forth. Interesting (though without any value) is the fact that

16

there are hundreds of names for the angels who perform these duties.

Their Classifications

Angels have rank. They are organized according to a careful system of authority. Some angels hold greater rank than others—that is, their office or position is higher than that of other angels. The words the Bible uses to demonstrate these classifications are listed below.

Daniel 4:13-23; 10:13, 20: messengers, princes, and chief princes.
1 Corinthians 15:24: power, dominion, and authority.
Ephesians 1:21; 3:10; 6:12: powers, dominion, authorities, and rulers.
Colossians 1:16; 2:10: powers, authorities, thrones, and rulers.
1 Thessalonians 4:16: archangel.
1 Peter 3:22: angels, authorities, and powers.
Jude 9: archangel.

There are other classifications, but these seem to more appropriately describe a different type of angelic creature altogether. These other angelic beings are called "cherubim" (the Bible refers to cherubim ninety-four times—e.g., Gen. 3:24), "seraphim" (mentioned only twice—Isa. 6:2, 6), and "living creatures" (recorded seventeen times in the Revelation; e.g., Rev. 4:6).

Their Characteristics

Angels are not like humans, except for the fact that they can take on a human form. There is never any illusion in the Word of God that these sacred agents are either baby-like or feminine or that they possess wings, concepts so often typified in Christmas cards and certain art forms. With the exception that cherubim and seraphim have two and three sets of wings respectively, these common notions have emerged and been sustained by artists alone. Angels are always portrayed in the Scriptures as strongly resembling the appearance of a man (Gen. 18:1-2 and 19:1-5).

Popular accounts of angels attest to their immense physical stature—over seven feet in height and weighing more than 400 pounds. That's impressive! But that, too, is without the clear and positive support of the Scriptures. The testimony of the Bible indicates that angels so naturally fit the normal human appearance that they can even be entertained as just another stranger, *"without knowing it"* (Heb. 13:2)!

These statements do not require, however, that all angels be "average" in size. Perhaps some are very big in contrast to humans. The scriptural evidence that is used to support this position is found in Genesis 6:1-4. In this passage we note that the sons of God married the daughters of men.

The result of this union were children who bore the designation of *nephilim*, which means "giants."

The argument for this position says that angels are called "sons of God" (Job 38:7), and that only this type of union would result in physical giants. Supporters of this view also find further confirmation in two New Testament passages which discuss the judgment of certain angels during the time period referred to in Genesis, chapter six (2 Pet. 2:4-5; Jude 5-7).

The argument against this position states that the "sons of God" refer to the godly men of the earth, who married the ungodly "daughters of men." The byproducts of this marriage were, presumably, giants of sin.

One of two choices presented, the former position seems to represent the more probable interpretation.

Here is a concise index of the normal characteristics that will be found in each angel:

1. Angels do not marry each other (Matt. 22:30).

2. Angels are physically stronger than humans (2 Pet. 2:11).

3. Angels are incapable of dying (Luke 20:35-36).

4. Angels have no need for rest (Rev. 4:8).

5. Angels possess a language that is distinct from any known language of earth (1 Cor. 13:1), though they seem to be quite capable of speaking any earthly language too. According to rabbinic lore, the angels speak Hebrew. It is supposed that

this was the language of the whole earth, prior to the confusion of tongues at Babel (Gen. 11). Obviously, this notion has no scriptural support.

6. Angels can travel at incalculable speeds, comparable at least to the speed of light (186,282 miles per second—Ezekiel 1:14).

7. Angels are *not* all-knowing. They are still increasing in their knowledge (1 Cor. 4:9; Eph. 3:10-11; 1 Pet. 1:12). One popular book on angels states that Gabriel has access to the timetable of everything that has been predicted except the second coming of Jesus Christ. This would seem to indicate a rather thorough knowledge. There is no scriptural evidence to support this claim. Angels are still involved in the learning process.

Their Names

If you think angels are named only in the Bible, think again. The sacred Scriptures provide the names for only two of these angelic beings— Michael (Dan. 10:21, 12:1; Jude 9; Rev. 12:7) and Gabriel (Dan. 8:15-27, 9:20-27; Luke 1:11-38). Outside the Bible, however, there are many other accounts of angels who bear specific names.

In extrabiblical sources there are complete lists of names for all of the archangels, ruling princes, throne angels, warden angels, governing angels, and so forth. There are literally hundreds upon hundreds of names for angels in pagan and secular accounts. God, on the other hand, is quite satisfied that we know only the names of two of these angels.

3

The Work of
Angels in Heaven

Some people have the unfortunate impression that angels don't have anything to do in heaven but ride on cushioned clouds and play golden harps. The conclusion drawn from this scene is that heaven must be a rather dull spot in the universe. But is this so? Indeed, it is not the case at all!

The Angels Worship

Angels aren't bored. They don't have to look around for something with which to amuse themselves. They are the most contented creatures in the universe (next, of course, to the jubilant and triumphant Christians who have gone up from this earth at the moment of their deaths to be forever in the exciting presence of Jesus).

One of the chief duties (and privileges) of the angels is to worship God. The Psalmist declares, *"Praise the Lord, you his angels . . . Praise the Lord, all his heavenly hosts"* (Ps. 103:20-21). Isaiah records how the seraphim, whom he saw orderly arranged above God's throne, called out the praises of God to each other saying, *"Holy, holy, holy is the Lord Almighty; the whole earth is full of his glory"* (Isa. 6:3). John records a similar note when he says, *"Day and night they [the living creatures] never stop saying: 'Holy, holy, holy is the Lord God Almighty, who was, and is, and is to come' "* (Rev. 4:8).

This service of the angels is not a lighthearted matter. It is sincere. The writer of the book of Hebrews declares that in heaven these angels are one *"joyful assembly"* (Heb. 12:22). There is no depression or boredom here. The heavenly hosts are excited. They love heaven and worship. We will too!

The Angels Work

The term "angel" serves to introduce us to their occupation. The word, in both Hebrew and Greek, means "a messenger" or "one who is sent in behalf of another." Angels, then, are God's servants—sometimes delivering messages to one person; at other times they direct the affairs of an entire nation.

Jesus states that the *"angels always see the face of my Father in heaven"* (Matt. 18:10). The idea suggested here is attentiveness for the purpose of action. The angels are eager to hear and fulfill God's orders. They are always standing close to God so they can respond immediately to His orders. There must be a great deal to do in the management of the whole universe. But God's special servants are up to the task.

4

The Work of Angels in the Sky

We often think of angels in their heavenly and earthly occupations, but we sometimes forget that they also perform a great deal of their works between these two realms. The sky—our own immediate atmosphere and outer space as well—is an important area of much angelic activity.

Angels Are Engaged in War

Not every angel who occupies a position in the sky is friendly. Some are hostile. There are good angels—those who are loyal to Christ. And there are bad angels—those who are pledged to follow Satan. This will be discussed more fully later. For the moment, however, let's examine how these two sets of angelic beings are engaged in combat with each other.

Daniel writes an interesting account of how an angel was dispatched from heaven in answer to one of his prayers. But before he could reach Daniel, the angel was stopped and held prisoner by an evil angel for twenty-one days. It wasn't until a higher ranking angel, "a chief prince," came that he was released to complete his mission (Dan. 10:12-11:1).

One of the intriguing works of angels often results from Christians' prayers. This is a very stimulating thought. It also is one full of insights, especially with regard to the seeming "slowness" of some answers to prayer. We are sometimes tempted to think our praying just never gets through. But this may not be the situation at all. As displayed in the episode with Daniel, his prayer was heard on the first day he prayed. An angel was sent in answer to his request that same day. The delay Daniel experienced wasn't due to any problem in his praying. Nor was the ear of the Lord in any degree closed to his request. Rather, the sole delay was demonic. Daniel's prayer answer was being withheld by an angelic enemy.

We must remember there is a war going on in the sky above us. Angels aren't being destroyed, but they are being hindered and sometimes rendered immobile. Until these temporarily defeated angels are assisted by other angels, especially by those angels of a superior status, they remain dormant. So, in the interim, let us follow Daniel's profound example and pray. Don't despair. The angels are fighting to give you God's answer, and they won't be delayed forever.

In the book of Revelation we read of a yet future *war in heaven*, when Michael (an archangel—Jude 9) and his angels will fight the devil and his angels. The outcome of this conflict will result in the total cleansing of the skies. All the evil angels will be cast to the earth for a brief period of great tribulation for earth's occupants, especially the Jews (Rev. 12:7-17). Later, this unholy company will be rounded up and dumped into the abyss (see Rev. 20 and Isa. 24:21-22). This is the meaning of Jesus' words when He says, regarding the events of the second coming, *"The stars [or angels] will fall from the sky, and the heavenly bodies [or angels] will be shaken"* (Matt. 24:29).

The greatest war of the skies is about to occur. It will have God's angels on the one front and Satan's angels on the other front. Not a single good angel will be harmed, and no evil angel will escape. It will be the most thorough conflict ever experienced in the angelic world.

For the moment we must remember that not everything in the sky is peaceful. It isn't. The angelic battles will continue until Jesus comes again. Satan is determined to undermine God's operations, but he will fail. The hosts of the Lord are on the winning side!

If you think angels are just singing in some heavenly choir, think again. They are fighters. Under Jesus' leadership, this body of spirit-beings is engaged in constant combat for the glory of God, the expansion of God's kingdom on earth, and the spiritual development of His followers.

Angelic Influence in Weather

Here is a mysterious realm but one we cannot reject or overlook. The angels are capable of participating in the forces of nature. For instance, they are said to be able to control the wind (Rev. 7:1), the seas, rivers and springs (Rev. 16:3-5, 12), and the intensity of the sun (Rev. 16:8-9).

Perhaps, when Jesus rebuked the winds and ordered the sea to become calm, He was actually commanding evil angels to release their hold on these natural elements (Mark 4:35-41). Rebuking violent storms may bring the same safety to us that it brought to Jesus and His disciples. We mustn't rule out such a possibility.

5

The Work of Angels
with Believers

One of the most comforting teachings in the entire Bible is the way angels work with believers.

Their Ministry of Protecting

Angels perform a broad range of protective services for the believer. Here is a threefold categorization of their activities in this area of ministry.

A. *Circumstantial Protection:* It is impossible to imagine how many times God's secret agents have protected us from what would have been called an "accident." There are no literal accidents, however. Think of it in this manner: God is all-knowing, all-present, all-powerful, and all-sovereign. Nothing can happen that is independent of

His awareness and ultimate permission. Accidents just don't happen (see Isa. 46:10-11 and Dan. 4:35). In fact, it is a certainty that *"All things work together for good to them that love God"* (Rom. 8:28 KJV).

The angels are actively engaged in protecting us from so-called accidents that do not fulfill God's plans. That's the reason for the Psalmist's elation when he writes, *"He [the Lord] will command his angels concerning you to guard you in all your ways"* (Ps. 91:11).

All of this does *not* imply that you will never have problems, for *"in this world you will have trouble"* (John 16:33). Jesus said so. But the trouble you will have will not touch you without first passing through the hands of God. And neither will you be confronted with circumstances that have escaped the angels' notice. They care too.

Corrie ten Boom tells of a time when she experienced angelic protection during her nightmare existence at Ravensbruck, a Nazi concentration camp. As she and her sister entered the prison everyone was told to completely undress and prepare to receive new clothing. But Corrie suddenly got the idea to hide her Bible in some woolen underwear. So, she rolled up the bundle, laid it in a corner, and prayed for the Lord to send His angels to help them.

After Corrie received her new outfit, she took the roll of underwear with the Bible and tucked it under her clothes. It created an obvious bulge, but she felt calmly assured that the angels would protect her.

Everyone in the building was to be checked twice before leaving. They were inspected in front, in back, and at both sides. Nothing unauthorized was to leave the room. As Corrie stepped up to the first checking point, the woman in front of her was caught hiding a wool vest. But she, next in line, was bypassed completely! Her sister, behind her, was thoroughly searched. At the second checking post the same thing happened again to Corrie. She was unnoticed! God's angels had taken her through the enemy's hands untouched!

B. *Physical Protection:* Our bodies are more frequently in trouble than we realize. But whether we are consciously facing physical harm or not, the angels are aware of our every plight. Consider, for instance, Shadrach, Meshach and Abednego. They were commanded to worship some ridiculous image, but they refused even though they were threatened with death by cremation. When the threats were ended, these three men were cast alive into a blazing furnace. It wasn't the time for their deaths, however, and God sent a special spirit-agent to protect them from the flames. They were miraculously preserved (Dan. 3).

Other examples of personal physical protection

are frequently recorded in the Bible. Hagar and her son, Ishmael, are protected from dying of thirst in the wilderness (Gen. 21:8-21). Isaac is saved from Abraham's knife because of an angel's voice (Gen. 22:1-12). Lot's family is delivered from sexual perverts and divine wrath by two angelic messengers (Gen. 19:1-29). Elisha is shielded from national foes by angels (2 Kings 6:8-23). Peter is guarded by the angels from a sadistic government official (Acts 12:5-11). Paul and his companions are preserved from perishing in a horrible shipwreck (Acts 27:9-44). Even Jesus is protected in the wilderness from the wild animals (Mark 1:13).

Billy Graham relates a story he heard when visiting our troops during the Korean War. A small band of Marines were trapped in a northern region of the cold country. The temperatures were twenty degrees below zero, and the men were about to freeze to death. They had not eaten anything for six days. The situation appeared hopeless.

One of the Marines was a Christian, and he taught the men some Scriptures, along with a song of worship. Shortly after singing this song, they noticed a wild boar rushing toward them. But suddenly he stopped, toppled over and died. That evening they ate a much-desired meal. The following day an English-speaking South Korean man approached them and led them back to safety.

When they went to thank him for saving their lives, he had completely disappeared!

C. *Demonic Protection:* Christians are not exempt from demonic attack, but we are empowered to overthrow these foes. James states it in this manner: *"Resist the devil, and he will flee from you"* (James 4:7). The word translated "resist" can also be rendered "stand fast." The Christian, then, can conquer Satan by boldly claiming God's promises for his or her own personal life.

There is no Christian who can defeat the devil by his own powers. No human can whip the devil. We're too weak. We're no match for his powers. But despite this statement, we can still command his departure from our midst. How is this accomplished? By trusting the Lord to keep His promises on your behalf. He sends His angels to defeat your demonic foes.

Paul states that we are in a constant struggle *"against the [evil, angelic] rulers, against the [demonic] authorities, against the [ungodly spirit] powers of this dark world and against the spiritual forces of evil in the heavenly realms"* (Eph. 6:12). His suggested remedy for the Christian is simple—put on the whole armor of God and then stand your ground (Eph. 6:13-19). There can be no doubt that angels honor our loyalty to these prerequisites for victory and secure for us a necessary spiritual triumph.

Their Ministry of Strengthening and Encouraging

How often we learn of believers—including the famous ones—who sense a real weakness or inability in themselves. Without the slightest doubt, the Holy Spirit gives to believers a power beyond our own natural abilities (see Acts 1:8 and 2 Tim. 1:7). Still, we sometimes feel very weak. And we just may be very weak.

We may become drained physically, emotionally, volitionally, domestically, vocationally and even spiritually. It is possible to cry out with the apostle Paul, I am *"under great pressure, far beyond [my] ability to endure, so that [I] despaired even of life"* (2 Cor. 1:8). This is not the mountaintop experience we are so accustomed to hearing about. Neither is it something we look forward to. But sometimes it comes, and when it arrives, we may need an angel to carry us through such a deep, but spiritual, valley.

Jesus experienced angelic strengthening no less than twice during His life. The first time occurred after He had fasted and been tempted by Satan for forty days. Matthew's record is quite plain. He simply says, *"the devil left him and angels came and attended him"* (Matt. 4:11). The word rendered "attended" means to minister, to serve, and to provide one's necessities. The precise activity here is not stated, but it seems reasonable that after this lengthy ordeal Jesus

36

needed strengthening for His entire body, soul and spirit. The angels supplied that need for Him.

The second time Jesus received help from the angels came on the night of His betrayal. He was in the garden praying. These were the darkest hours of Jesus' entire life. With great agony He faced the cruel tests that were soon to encompass Him. The pressure of the moment was so intense that Jesus actually perspired droplets of blood.

Where is help to be found in such difficulty? The answer is, the ministry of angels. It was during this, the bleakest moment of Jesus' life, that *an angel from heaven appeared to him and strengthened him*" (Luke 22:43)!

Jesus needed the ministry of angels. And He found their works most satisfying.

Some friends of mine were pressed hard by a series of difficulties. They were facing the greatest struggles of their lives when something happened that gave them support for the duration of their tests. On two occasions an angel appeared and assured them that God would get them through their dark tunnel. With those few words they straightened their backs, squared their shoulders, and triumphantly pressed on. In the end, after several more painful weeks, they emerged as much more stable and optimistic believers.

Their Ministry of Guiding

God utilizes a grand variety of ways for giving

guidance to His people—the Scriptures (first and foremost), dreams, visions, circumstances, people, gifts of the Spirit, inner peace, His audible voice, His inner voice in the believer's spirit, and, of course, angels.

When the faithful female disciples of Christ approached His tomb on that first Easter Sunday, it was an angel who told them where they were to go and what they were to say (Matt. 28:5-7). An angel told Philip, "*Go south to the road—the desert road—that goes down from Jerusalem to Gaza*" (Acts 8:26). That's being pretty specific. The result was the conversion and baptism of an important official in Ethiopia. Cornelius, a short while later, was directed by another angel to send for Peter and to have him come and tell the gospel story (Acts 10). The outcome is further conversions, along with the outpouring of the Holy Spirit. Approximately thirty years after this event Paul is told by an angel that he "*must stand trial before Caesar*" (Acts 27:23-24). The news was both comforting and confirming. Without a doubt this additional revelation gave a greater boldness to Paul and a deeper joy in his Lord.

Various persons today attest to this type of guidance with subsequent opportunities for witnessing. This is thrilling. On the other hand, some people are having unusual visitations without any meaningful or fruitful byproducts. This kind of revelation is most questionable. We will expose such matters carefully at a later point.

Their Ministry of Instructing

The word "angel" means "messenger." Naturally this implies that they act as God's postmen, delivering pieces of information that are given to them by Him. In the Scriptures angels communicate two kinds of data: the impartation of revelations, and the interpretation of revelations. Let's consider these individually.

A. *Impartation of Revelations:* By "revelations" I mean special, divinely ordered information, especially with regard to future events, which by design is to be incorporated into the sacred canon of Scripture. There is no shortage of such experiences recorded in the Scriptures.

Paul writes that *"the law [probably the Ten Commandments] was put into effect through angels"* (Gal. 3:19). In other words, the message which Moses received on Mount Sinai was actually *"spoken by angels"* (Heb. 2:2; cf. Acts 7:38, 53). Often God's message is delivered by an angelic mediator—one who goes in His place.

The entire book of the Revelation is the result of angelic messages. John says, *"He [Jesus Christ] made it [the revelation] known by sending his angel to his servant John"* (Rev. 1:1). Major parts of the book of Daniel owe their existence to angelic revelations (see 7:13ff, 8:15ff, 9:20ff, 10:1-12:13). The writings of Zechariah are heavily packed with angelic conversations (see Zech. 1:9, 13, 14, 19; 2:3; 4:1, 4, 5; 5:5; 6:4-5).

In the New Testament, it was an angel that foretold to Zechariah the pregnancy of his wife and the subsequent birth of John the Baptist (Luke 1:11-20). The same angel told Mary about her miraculous conception of the child Jesus (Matt. 1:20-25; Luke 1:26-35). Angels appeared to the shepherds of Bethlehem, telling them of the Savior's birth and where they could find Him (Luke 2:8-12).

The data is ample. But much confusion has arisen through a misunderstanding of this kind of revelation. It has been supposed that God is still talking today precisely as He did to those persons and periods mentioned above. There is, however, a very dangerous flaw in this notion. Some persons have accepted the messages brought to them by angelic messengers without realizing that the time for issuing new revelations for the world is past. At the risk of sounding anti-supernatural (which I am not!) let me firmly declare that the period for canon-type revelations (that is, revelations that are binding for the universal Church) stopped when the New Testament Scriptures were completed.

Do not lose me here. These statements do not grieve "the Spirit of truth" (John 16:13). It is error that grieves God. And we could possibly soon find ourselves in the thick of it if we start accepting

40

revelations that go beyond the final and ultimate standard of the Scriptures. The entire Mormon church, for instance, has its roots in extrabiblical revelations that were delivered by an angel, supposedly from the heart of God!

Certain teachers today are publishing revelations and prophecies. These are then distributed to a large circle of readers who live all over the world. Sometimes such writings have immense value and are worthy of the widest possible circulation. But the opposite is also true. Many so-called revelations from God smack solely of prosperity pacts and bless-me bundles. Further, the language that is used is often universal-sounding (example: "My plan for the earth is . . ."; or "My will for all believers is . . ."). The reader is given the impression that this contemporary, right-from-heaven word-from-the-Lord is every bit as authoritative for the entire Body of Christ as the forever-settled, written Word of God, the Bible. But this *cannot* be the actual case.

If God were speaking today exactly as He spoke during the early years of the Church, then these messages should be bound and laid alongside the writings of the New Testament and bound together to be followed with the rest of the "words from God." Each year an updated Bible should be issued in order to keep up with the latest word from heaven. I'm sincere; if God hasn't changed His methods at all, then we ought to never consider our Bibles as being complete—not until the second of the Lord's return to this earth. *But no sensible Christian can accept this ridiculous notion, though many seem to be doing just this.*

No one, no matter how sensational, glorious or warming, is receiving new truth (or new Scripture) from God. Insights, yes. Canon, never. The early work, the foundational labors, are forever laid. We build the local church and individual Christian lives *upon* it; we add *nothing* to this base. No further universally binding revelations for the canon are needed (see Eph. 2:19-3:5).

Paul is emphatic when he states, ". . . *if we or an angel from heaven should preach a gospel [that is, a proclamation regarding any aspect of the kingdom of God] other than the one we preached to you, let him be eternally condemned! As we have already said, so now I say again: If anybody is preaching to you a gospel other than what you accepted, let him be eternally condemned!"* (Gal. 1:8-9).

All of this warning is given with one intent: beware of false angelic messages and untrue prophecies or preachings. I am not endeavoring to discount the reality or the value of these experiences, but to merely serve notice that not every so-called supernatural experience or utterance bearing God's name is actually from Him.

Remember Matthew 7:21-23. " *'Not everyone*

who says to me, "Lord, Lord," will enter the kingdom of heaven, but only he who does the will of my Father who is in heaven. Many will say to me on that day, "Lord, Lord, did we not prophesy in your name, and in your name drive out demons and perform many miracles?" Then I will tell them plainly, "I never knew you. Away from me, you evildoers!" ' "

B. *Interpretation of Revelations:* In the Scriptures when someone received a revelation, especially a prophetic vision, he would often be perplexed at the meaning of what he saw. At these points an angel would interpret the scene.

This happened on several occasions to Daniel, Zechariah and John. The visions they received were devoid of meaning. So they would have their understanding enriched by the additional comments provided by an attending angel (see Dan. 7:13ff, 8:15ff, 9:20ff, 10:1-12:13; Zech. 1:9, 2:3, 4:1, 5:5, 6:4-5; Rev. 7:9-17; etc.).

Currently we have heard of angels who are, in effect, conducting a series of topical Bible studies. Supposedly the insights derived from such encounters are of unsurpassed value. According to these reports it would be impossible to have gained these great truths if it were not for the words delivered by the angelic messengers.

There are no less than two crippling problems presented with this kind of experience. First, it is highly unlikely (I'm inclined to say "unthinkable") that certain segments of God's Word can only be understood after being tutored by an angel. This would make the Bible a closed book, except, of course, for those who have had these angelic teaching sessions, or for those who are "privileged" to sit at the feet of one who has received these angelic studies.

Second, there is little support from the testimony of Scripture that angels conduct Bible studies (except the unique kind of instruction that is stated above, which usually accompanies a vision itself). It is more in keeping with the Bible to conclude that the ministry of teaching is confined to the Holy Spirit and to those gifted by that same Spirit to do teaching (see Rom. 12:6-7; 1 John 2:20, 27). These statements are not intended to rule out the fact that an angel can appear to someone and give to him or her helpful comments, but it seems highly unlikely that these comments will take the shape of a detailed Bible study so that you might understand heretofore unfathomable treasures.

Their Ministry of Chastisement

Here is a truth that has not found worldwide acceptance among Christians (particularly in America). It is the matter of chastisement. With such a current overemphasis on the teaching of love (including God's love), it is not surprising that some should reject the idea that God also disciplines His children. But the record of Scripture is clear on this point: ". . . *do not make light of the Lord's discipline . . . the Lord disciplines those he loves, and he punishes everyone he accepts as a son. . . . God disciplines us for our good, that we might share in his holiness*" (Heb. 12:5-10).

How does God administer chastisement or discipline? Does He come to each one of us individually and deal with us according to our ways? This is doubtful. It is much more likely that the angels have this responsibility.

In the book of 1 Chronicles we read how David was enticed by Satan to count all the available men who could fight for the king. This numbering amounted to David openly displaying doubt that the Lord's army would defend Israel, as well as pride in his own natural resources. So God decided that David should be chastened for this public display of distrust and pride. The result was the dispatching of an angel to put a plague on Israel (1 Chron. 21:1-30; see also 2 Sam. 24). The price of David's sin was most costly. It was a terrible lesson, but one David was to have branded into him by a chastening angel.

It doesn't seem at all out of line to suggest that the chastisement discussed in 1 Corinthians 11:27-34 is also administered by God's angels. Here we find certain believers sitting at the Lord's Supper who have shown a gross disrespect for His body (which probably refers to both their carefree attitude for the literal body of Christ, and their inconsiderate attitude for the mystical Body of Christ—the local church).

The outcome for their laxness is the Lord's chastisement—some are made weak, others are made sick, and still others are even put to sleep (or death). All of this was accomplished so that they would "not be condemned with the world" (1 Cor. 11:32). We mustn't overlook the effect that is produced by our sins. The same angels who are present to protect us may also be used to spank us. Beware.

Their Ministry of Answering Prayer

It should be obvious by this point that angels are mediators between heaven and earth. God does not literally move His presence from one spot to another in order to answer prayer requests. Rather, He hears our prayers in heaven and then sends forth an appropriate answer in the hands of an angel.

This statement is brought forth most brilliantly to us by an experience recorded in the writings of Daniel. For twenty-one days he prayed. On the twenty-first day his answer arrived—via an angel. Another interesting account is found in Acts 12:1-17, when the early church prayed for Peter's release from prison. In answer to this request an angel was ordered to release Peter from this bondage.

46

Their Ministry to the Dying

In a very moving story of the details of the deaths of two totally different men, Jesus describes the passing from this life to our future abode (whether it be the righteous dead who go to paradise [prior to the resurrection] or the unrighteous ones who go to hades). The exciting part of the episode focuses upon Lazarus, a beggar, who died and was carried by the angels into Abraham's bosom (Luke 16:22). If Lazarus was like most of us he never saw a single angel during his whole lifetime. But at the moment of his death, when his spirit was departing from his body, he could clearly behold the angelic world. His spirit met God's ministering spirits. This is such a comforting thought. The first thing our spiritual eyes will envision at the moment of our deaths is the extended arms of God's angels, who will whisk us immediately into the presence of Jesus (see also 2 Cor. 5:8; Phil. 1:21-23).

It is quite reasonable to imagine that the unrighteous dead are also carried by God's host to their place of torment. This trip for them, understandably, is no pleasure ride.

Guardian Angels in General

The writer to the Hebrews declares, *"Are not all angels ministering spirits sent to serve those who will inherit salvation?"* (Heb. 1:14). The term "salvation" is employed here in a three-tense manner: past (justification), present (sanctification), and future (glorification). Angels are sent to those who will someday be glorified and be changed into the image of Christ (1 John 3:2).

Jesus informed His audience to not look down in a negative manner on the children who had gathered about Him. Why? Because "*their angels in heaven always see the face of my Father*," said Jesus (Matt. 18:10). In other words, kids are important to angels too.

There can be no mistake about this. Christians are under the guardianship of the angels (plural). Whether or not we have the same one(s) all of our lives is not stated and is unimportant. But one thing is certain—they are about us now, and others are before God awaiting His next orders on our behalf. This is encouraging!

Angelic Appearances in General

Very few persons have had the privilege of consciously seeing an angel. The following people (thirty-two individuals or groups) are said to have seen angels:

1. Hagar—twice (Gen. 16:7-11; 21:17)
2. Abraham—three times (Gen. 18:2; 22:11, 15)
3. Lot (Gen. 19:1-22)
4. Jacob—three times (Gen. 28:12; 31:11; 32:1)
5. Moses (Exod. 3:2)
6. Balaam (Num. 22:22-35)
7. Joshua (Josh. 5:13-15)

8. Israel (Judg. 2:1-5)
9. Gideon (Judg. 6:11)
10. Manoah's wife (Judg. 13:3-5)
11. Manoah and his wife (Judg. 13:9-21)
12. David (2 Sam. 24)
13. Elijah—four times (1 Kings 19:5-7; 2 Kings 1:3, 15)
14. Elisha and servant (2 Kings 6:16-17)
15. Assyrians (2 Kings 19:35)
16. Shadrach, Meshach, and Abednego (Dan. 3)
17. Nebuchadnezzar (Dan. 3)
18. Daniel—five times (Dan. 6:22; 8:15-16; 9:20-21; 10:5; 12:5)
19. Zechariah—seven times (Zech. 1:8-19; 2:3; 3:1-6; 4:1-5; 5:5-10; 6:4-5; 12:8)
20. Joseph—three times (Matt. 1:20; 2:13, 19)
21. Mary (Luke 1:26-38)
22. Zechariah (Luke 1:11-20)
23. Shepherds (Luke 2:9-14)
24. Jesus—twice (Matt. 4:11; Luke 22:43)
25. Women at tomb (Matt. 28:1-5)
26. Disciples (Acts 1:10-11)
27. Peter and John (Acts 5:19)
28. Philip (Acts 8:26)
29. Cornelius (Acts 10:3)
30. Peter (Acts 12:7-11)
31. Paul (Acts 27:23)
32. John (Rev. 1:1)

Several observations ought to be noted regarding

the general nature of the data.

First, the angelic visitations are unevenly divided over the 2,100-year biblical period. There are showings in all the stages of Israel's history: Theocratic period—Abraham to David (appearances to eleven people); Monarchical period—David to the Exile (appearances to four people), Hierarchical period—the Exile to Christ (appearances to four people), and the New Testament period (appearances to thirteen people).

Second, the angelic visitations are really quite rare—only nineteen occurrences in the 2,000-year Old Testament period, and thirteen during the 100-year founding period of the New Testament Church. There certainly cannot be said to be any frequency of angelic appearances during the biblical era.

Third, the angels rarely revisited anyone. Zechariah, who tallies the greatest number of angelic visits—seven—probably received them over a short two-year period. Daniel, next in line, with five appearances, also seems to have seen the angels in a fairly short period of his life. The same could be said of the majority of the six persons who in 2,100 years ever had more than a single angelic visit. In each of the other twenty-six cases the angels only showed up once.

Fourth, the angels virtually never appeared unless there was some rare circumstance to warrant their unprecedented arrival. Often the appearances resulted in a special rescue mission (whether it be physical or spiritual). Also, frequently the cause was to impart some canon-type revelation regarding a recent prophetic vision. In short, the angelic encounters of the Bible are never commonplace or casual. There is always something special entailed in their appearing. They never seem to appear just to bless the one receiving the visit. The cause is always greater.

When a person today attests to numerous encounters with the spirit world, certain warning flags are raised. No one, in 2,100 years of biblical history, ever could say that he had numerous encounters with angels. They are rare events. And often they are associated with a crisis or singularly spectacular event. These above insights must be kept in mind when evaluating any current reports of angelic encounters.

6

The Work of Angels with Unbelievers

We are naturally inclined to believe God's angels work exclusively with the saved, and that Satan's angels work only with the lost. But this is doubly wrong. Good angels often work with bad people, and bad angels often work with good people. The occupations of the evil angels will be discussed later. For the moment, let us consider how God's holy angels work with unholy people.

They Execute Temporary Judgments

In the previous chapter we noted how God's angels are used to chastise His followers when they fail to repent of their sins. Now we will discover how these same angels can bring a similar act of judgment against non-Christians too.

Lot lived in a wicked city. The people there were deeply engrossed in a multitude of vices. Among the sins listed against these persons is homosexuality. There can be no doubt concerning the Lord's attitude with regard to this evil— He sent two angels to rescue Lot and his family, and then to destroy the entire community for its horrible corruption.

In the process of the rescue operation these two male angels are approached by certain male members of the population who had an interest in having sexual relations with them. The response of the two angels to this gesture is immediate—*"they struck the men . . . with blindness"* (see Gen. 19:1-13). The repulsive overture on the part of the gays was met with an execution of divine justice.

Some years later, at a critical point in Israel's history, a false prophet was hired to predict the ruin of this tiny nation. The profiting prophet's name was Balaam. He had little interest in helping God's people, so he consented. But the Lord wouldn't allow this false spokesman to utter anything but a blessing upon Israel. Through the use of an angelic messenger Balaam was compelled to speak God's words. Certainly this powerful and positive speech served to protect the small nation of Jews from her treacherous and selfishly ambitious neighbors (Num. 22:21-24:25).

The ten plagues that fell on the people of Egypt were delivered by angels (Ps. 78:41-55). The plague of the water turning to blood, the overnight population explosion of the frogs, the irritating swarms of gnats, the disturbingly high number of flies, the sudden sickness and death of Egypt's livestock, the festering boils upon the people's bodies, the worst hailstorm in Egypt's history, the unstoppable blanket of devouring locusts, the utter darkness for three days and nights, and finally, the death of all the first-born males—each had an angelic base (Exod. 7:14-11:10).

Evil men are not "living it up" all the time. The way of the world is not as blissful as it appears on the surface. Sin, whether committed by saints or sinners, will not escape God's notice or discipline.

The Christian is not without earthly foes. The speech and action of those who oppose the Christian faith can often spell the difference between a victory or defeat for us and our work. The extension and edification of God's kingdom can be temporarily thwarted by carnal persons. So, when this happens, God dispatches a company of angelic messengers. We can be assured that the parade of evil men and women who oppose the gospel of Christ are on the angels' watch list. And when God says it is time for the evil practices to cease, they will be stopped.

The world would be a far worse place if it were not for the judgments administered by the angels.

They Execute Permanent Judgments

Any judgment inflicted by the angels is severe, and it is obvious that some of their works are of a permanent nature. For instance, when Herod proudly received the praises of his audience, and refused to honor God, *"an angel struck him down, and he was eaten by worms and died"* (Acts 12:23)!

The death of some people is clearly premature. Some people who die early are rebellious, arrogant and destructive. Some, in God's plans, are permitted a full age, even though they are sinners. But to others, a fatal sentence is carried out before they reach their intended maturity. To such persons the angels are sent to remove them from this life.

Sin is expensive, period. And those who think they can stiff-arm God to the outer edges of their lives and escape His judgments had better think again. The angels are watching, and when they are assigned an order to execute judgment toward the sinner, their mission will be fulfilled.

They Clear the Path for Our Conversion

The angels find great pleasure in the conversion of a sinner. They don't delight in seeing people needing judgment. They would much rather bless than judge. Jesus said, *"I tell you, there is rejoicing in the presence of the angels of God over one sinner who repents"* (Luke 15:10). It seems highly improbable to assume that the angels play no role in clearing the path for people to receive Jesus Christ as their Lord and Savior. The opposite appears to be far more accurate. Angels *do* assist in bringing us to salvation.

One may well wonder just how God's angels aid the sinner in his or her acceptance of Christ. Perhaps it is safe to say this much. Satan's angels are busy maintaining a blindfold over the spiritual eye of all nonbelievers (2 Cor. 4:3-4). It is reasonable to assume that God sends His angels to at least occasionally overpower these evil forces and to remove these spiritual blinders, giving people an opportunity to see God's light for personal deliverance from sin, self and Satan.

The writer to the Hebrews says that the angels are sent *"to serve those who will inherit salvation"* (Heb. 1-14). Among other things, it seems fair to say that this verse encompasses enough breadth to include the ministry of God's angels with those who are currently lost but will eventually become saved.

Rejoice, Christians. God and His angels were working with you before you ever surrendered your life to Him. The thought of being a disciple of Jesus Christ may have been, for the most part, the farthest thing from your mind. But the Lord had you, all the time, on His heart. And He sent His angels to minister to you despite your unbelief and self-willed living.

These statements must also be permitted to encourage us to pray for our lost loved ones and associates. These prayers are not resting idle in heaven. Rather, God hears our prayers, and He sends forth angels to provide opportunities for those mentioned in our prayers to hear the message of personal salvation through Jesus Christ! Be assured that God acts upon these intercessory concerns. He cares for the lost as much (and far more!) than any one of us can possibly care. (Be certain to read Revelation 14:6-13 on the future work of three angels in proclaiming the eternal gospel of salvation.)

7

The Work of Angels in Cities and Nations

Whenever angels are engaged in the concerns that touch individual lives, it becomes evident that they are also actively involved in the issues that touch a broader collection of people, namely cities and nations. In other words, angels have a pluralistic ministry, as well as a private and personal one. Their works can take on a distinctively city-wide or nationwide role. The insights to be gleaned from this aspect of the angels' activities must capture our attention.

Their Role in Government

The first indication we have of angelic involvement on the national level is seen in the book of Exodus. Here we find the angel of the

Lord speaking to Moses from a burning bush (Exod. 3). The gist of the conversation concerns the deliverance of the Hebrew people (who are practically a nation in the midst of Egypt's land). The promises made to Moses here were literally fulfilled. Notice, however, in the success of this remarkable feat, is an angel who went before them to assure its accomplishment (see Exod. 14:19; 23:20). Israel escaped Egypt's clutch and was able to gain her national independence because of an angel's aid.

In subsequent Scripture references we learn God has assigned specific angels to watch over the affairs of national Israel. This principal assignment has fallen to *"Michael, the great prince who protects [Israel's] people"* (Dan. 12:1). Serving this *"archangel"* (Jude 9) are a company of lesser ranking angels (Rev. 12:7—*"Michael and his angels. . ."*). Together, they work to assure the achievement of certain national interests.

A fascinating truth emerging from these statements is found in the fact that Israel is not alone in possessing what might be called "national angels" (or angels with national, governmental responsibilities). In the book of Daniel we read of the angelic *"prince of the Persian kingdom"* (Dan. 10:13). This is an evil angel! Again, we read of *"the prince of Greece,"* who is also a high-ranking evil angel (Dan. 10:20).

These national angels, then, may be either

from God or from Satan. It seems evident that above each nation on this earth presides a heavenly host. In some cases these archangels will be holy; in other instances they will be unholy powers. From their lofty platform, these angels await orders from their respective commanders-in-chief (either Jesus or Satan). They are then directed to influence the course of a nation.

We might be tempted to think that both men and nations control their own destinies. But this is only partially true. The establishment, expansion and/or decline of each nation—in all of time—owes its history to God and to the angels who preside over them.

Paul affirms these statements in this profound manner: *"The God who made the world and everything in it is the Lord. . . . And he is not served by human hands, as if he needed anything, because he himself gives all men life and breath and everything else. For from one man he made every nation of men . . . and he determined the times set for them and the exact places where they should live"* (Acts 17:24-26)!

The data is sufficient. God's angels (and Satan's angels too) have political ties.

Their Role in City and National Judgments

Just as surely as God's angels effect judgment against individual sinners, they, too, express

God's wrath in judging whole cities and even entire nations. There is no shortage of examples of this.

The cities of Sodom and Gomorrah were so utterly crushed by angels that to this day we still haven't discovered their remains (though it is thought by current scholarship that the site of these ancient ruins can be found beneath the waters at the south end of the Dead Sea—see Genesis 19).

In a single night the angel of the Lord killed 185,000 Assyrian soldiers who were posing a serious threat to Israel (2 Kings 19:35). In Joshua's campaign against Jericho he was notified by the commander of the Lord's angelic army that the angel would have more to do with Joshua's triumph than he might otherwise have supposed.

Derek Prince tells the story of how he and his wife prayed for Israel during the conflict with the Arabs in 1948. At that time Derek and his wife lived in Jerusalem, the heart of the battle. The Jewish soldiers were outnumbered ten to one; still it seemed that the enemy was paralyzed to do anything against them. Finally, Israel's independence was settled. The point Mr. Prince makes in this story is that their specific prayers were answered to the very letter. The Princes were overwhelmingly convinced that God himself had brought about this seemingly impossible victory. Without a doubt the source for this victory can be attributed to prayer and the working of national angels!

George Otis relates almost identical reports of angelic miracles in the most recent Israeli-Arab conflict. In this confrontation, the enemy of Israel was often perplexed; for instance, they would see more tanks than were actually present. Their warfare strategy was confounded, and as a result they lost what should have been easy victories. The angels, according to Mr. Otis, defended the tiny nation of Israel from her big neighbors, just as they did in Bible times!

Other stories and scriptural references could be cited in support of these statements, but no further elaboration is necessary. However, there is a side to these episodes we have yet to see. It is the aspect of angelic withdrawal.

Their Role in City and National Chastisement

God's angels do not always protect God's people. Sometimes, because of unrepentant sin on the part of God's children, He is compelled to chastise the cities of the nations He normally protects.

For instance, the angel of the Lord told the nation of Israel, shortly after her miraculous escape from Egypt, that because of disobedience He would no longer uproot her enemies before her (Judg. 2:1-3)! This is angelic withdrawal.

It is a shocking thought that angels can withdraw their guardianship. God's national angels would only guard Israel as she walked in harmony with His will for them. When she failed to serve the Lord properly, then He suspended the services of the angels in charge of her national security. In fact, some biblical references go so far as to state that God's angels will turn their former sword of protection into a weapon of chastisement upon the Father's disobedient children (see 2 Sam. 24:15-16).

There can be no hesitation on our part to see a most practical point throughout all of this information. The truths are all too evident. We in America have been tremendously blessed by the Lord. He has watched over us through His angelic national guards. We have been safe and secure. But can we assume this same protection and privilege will last forever?

The answer to this vital question is "yes" or "no"—depending on America's righteousness. God *will* shield us *if* we will honor and magnify Him, as a national interest. However, *if* we, as a nation, will not submit to the Lordship of Christ, then He *will not* protect us any more than He protected Israel in her periods of disobedience! The choice is ours—guardianship for submission or chastisement for insubordination. America, beware!

8

The Angel of the Lord ˒

There is a very great difference among the angels. They vary from each other in their creation, power and function. Often the distinctions are quite pronounced, but the uniqueness of one angel in particular exceeds all others. He is *the angel of the Lord.* He stands alone among the heavenly host.

The Five Bodies of Jesus

It is sometimes difficult for us to imagine that Jesus ever really existed prior to His appearance in the Gospel accounts. We tend to imagine that though He is, was, and will ever be God, that for some reason He didn't play a very significant role, if any role at all, during the entire Old

Testament period. But this notion is clearly erroneous. Jesus was exceedingly active before His mysterious and magnificent conception in Mary's womb.

When we think of a body, we are prone to envision only a physical one like our own. We may even suppose that for each person there has been assigned only one body. But this is not the case at all. For instance, each believer will experience three distinct forms (or bodies): (1) the initial form—from birth to death; (2) the intermediate form—from death to the great resurrection; and (3) the permanent form—from the great resurrection forward throughout all of eternity. The first body is physical, the second is spiritual, and the third is glorified (see 1 Cor. 15; 2 Cor. 5:1-8).

It should not be difficult—in view of this fact—to recognize that Jesus, too, has known different bodies at various points in the development of His special life. Let us consider the five bodies of Jesus.

1. *His Spiritual Body:* Jesus is God. Jesus is man. In His deity He is eternal, without beginning or end. But in His humanity He is only everlasting—with a definite beginning, though without any end. As God, Jesus is changeless. As man, however, Jesus has changed greatly.

Paul writes this commentary on the first body, as well as the subsequent body, of Jesus Christ.

"Who [Jesus], being in very nature [or form] God, did not consider equality with God something to be grasped [as if he needed something he didn't possess]" (Phil. 2:6).

Jesus is the unique member of the Trinity. Originally Jesus shared the same "nature" or form and essence of the other parties in the Trinity. They were each Spirit. But Jesus changed. He took on new forms.

2. *His Physical Body:* As Paul continues his discussion on the tremendous lowliness of our Lord, he states that He "*made himself nothing, taking the very nature [or form] of a servant, being made in human likeness*" (Phil. 2:7).

When did Jesus take on this "human likeness"? Immediately we are guided by instinct to a crude stall and a manger scene. Here we see Jesus—God in the flesh. But is this the very beginning of Jesus' humanity? Probably not. Let's go back in time for a moment. Let's go back to the creation of the earth. Here are two passages from God's Word to serve as our guide:

"*Then God said, 'Let us make man in our image, in our likeness.' . . . So God created man in his own image, in the image of God he created him*" (Gen. 1:26-27).

"*Then the man and his wife heard the sound of the Lord God as he was walking in the garden in the cool of the day, and they hid from the Lord God among the trees of the garden*" (Gen. 3:8).

It is certain that there is a need for caution here. We must guard against placing a pound of emphasis upon a mere ounce of truth. Nevertheless, it seems evident that at least two simple observations may be deduced from these passages.

(a) Because the record of Jesus' first physical body predates the Gospel narratives of His birth to the Virgin Mary, it is also entirely conceivable that His physical appearance also predates the creation of Adam and Eve. In other words, when God said, "Let *us* make man in *our* image, in *our* likeness . . .," the intent may well have been to make mankind with not only certain inner features after God's resemblance (such as moral, intellectual and volitional aspects), but also certain outer features that were characteristic of Jesus' physical frame (cf. Gen. 5:1-3 with James 3:9).

(b) In order for God to walk in the garden with Adam and Eve, it only seems natural that He should appear to them in human form, even as He did to Abraham years later (Gen. 18:1-2). Since two members of the Godhead are explicitly said to be "Spirit" (John 4:24), and never seen by the human eye (John 1:18), it quite logically follows that Jesus, in his pre-Bethlehem body, walked and talked with the first couple.

Jesus had a physical body in both the Old and the New Testaments. He walked with men of both epochs.

3. *His Glorified Body:* Jesus died. God never died. The Holy Spirit never died. But the humanity of Jesus grew weak, and in terrible anguish, He ceased to live. On the cross, bearing the sins of the whole world for all of time, Jesus experienced physical death. Following this, He was buried. But something happened. He awoke! He arose! The empty tomb proclaims His power over death.

Jesus did the impossible. He conquered death. He arose from its grips a new man—a glorified man, a man with a new body of immortality and incorruption. Paul writes, *"We eagerly await a Savior from there [heaven], the Lord Jesus Christ, who, by the power that enables him to bring everything under his control, will transform our lowly bodies so that they will be like his glorious body"* (Phil. 3:20). This is the third body of Jesus. There are two more. (For further details on the glorified body see 1 Cor. 15; 2 Cor. 5:1-8; and John 20:19-20, 26-28.)

4. *His Christian Body:* The title for this point is not fully descriptive of its meaning. The actual idea is this. Jesus inhabits the body of each genuine Christian. Jesus himself gives us this information. *"I will not leave you as orphans; I will come to you. . . . On that day you will realize that I am in my Father, and you are in me, and I am in you"* (John 14:18-20; also, v. 23).

69

This magnificent truth is far beyond our intellectual comprehension. Jesus is surely seated at the right hand of the Father in heaven (in one sense); yet He also dwells within every single loving and obedient Christian (in another sense). We can be thankful that our experiencing this fact is not conditioned by our first understanding it. The promise is true. The reality is genuine. And the experience is what we need to assist us in becoming more like Him who indwells us (see Rom. 8:29; Gal. 4:19).

5. *His Church Body:* This is a familiar truth, though its implications have yet to reach most of us. Jesus is more than *in* the local church; He *is* the local church as well. Paul says, *"Now you are the body of Christ, and each one of you is a part of it "* (1 Cor. 12:27). The meaning of this expression is multiple.

(a) The local church (and obviously, thereby, the universal Church) owes it existence to Jesus. If Jesus had not come there would be no Church.

(b) The local church derives its leadership from its Head, Jesus Christ. Where His headship is not in control, then to the corresponding degree there can be no true expression of His body.

(c) The local church requires the functioning of all its parts (that is, each Christian) before it can exhibit the full stature of Christ. When this is achieved, however, it is safe to assert that this local church will reflect the full stature of Christ himself (Eph. 4:11-16)! It is God's aim that attending church today should be no different from attending a meeting conducted by Jesus himself. As profound and powerful as this sounds, we might think it is quite unrealistic, but our very designation—*The Body of Christ*—calls us to accept this wonderful standard.

All of the above discussion has been presented with one prominent aim—to lay the foundation for the fact that references to the angel of the Lord are actually references to the pre-incarnate body of Jesus (number 2 above). Below are some clear proofs for this assertion.

The Angel of the Lord Is Jesus

The angel of the Lord is no ordinary angel. Some writers say this angel is Michael; others say he is Gabriel, Chrioni, Uriel and Remiel. But consider these unique statements that accompany this angel's appearances.

1. When Hagar became lost in the wilderness, the angel of the Lord found and rescued her. In the same breath, Moses, who wrote this account, said it was the Lord himself who spoke with her (Gen. 16:7, 13).

2. When Moses encountered the burning bush, it was the angel of the Lord who is said to have spoken with him. Later, however, the wording shifts to indicate that it was "God" and the "Lord" who was doing the speaking, as if all three were

one in the same person (Exod. 3:1-14).

3. When Gideon was commissioned to serve Israel, the recruitment is said to have taken place by the angel of the Lord, who is, again, also called the Lord (Judges 6:12, 14).

4. When Manoah and his wife saw the angel of the Lord, they feared they would die because they believed they had seen God himself (Judges 13:21-22).

5. Of the three members of the Godhead, only Jesus has served as the visible expression of God (John 1:14, 18). The Father is Spirit (John 4:24). The Holy Spirit is Spirit. The only member of the Trinity who is not now Spirit is Jesus.

These proofs are self-evident. Perhaps, however, there is one more point requiring our attention. Did you know that the angel of the Lord cannot be found outside the Old Testament? All the references to the angel of the Lord in the New Testament are inaccurate translations of the Greek (which, by the way, only appear in the King James Version of the Bible— later translations have caught this translation error). Each New Testament rendering should read, "*an* angel of the Lord," making the reference to any one of a numberless host.

The angel of the Lord is unique. He is the Jesus of the Old Testament. For further insights, read these references: Gen. 21:17, 22:11, 15; Num. 22:22ff; Judges 5:23; 6:11ff; 13:3ff; 1 Kings 19:5ff; 2 Kings 1:3ff, 19:35; 1 Chron. 21:12ff; and Isa. 37:36.

PART II

SATAN

9

The Rise and Fall of Satan

The devil has not always existed. Neither has the devil always been the devil. Originally he was among the good angels, but he rebelled and led a vast number of other angels with him in a revolt against God. In these pages we will explore the rise and fall of Satan and his host. The insights to be gleaned from this epoch are intensely practical.

The Original State of Satan

When God created the earth and the heavens (which naturally include the angels), He pronounced His approval upon the entire universe by saying, "*it was very good*" (Gen. 1:31). There was no evil present—none. All of the angels were ministering in harmony with God's will. Adam and Eve were without sin. Everything was perfect.

Among the angelic host there was not a thought of anarchy. They recognized Jesus as their Creator and Lord (John 1:3; Col. 1:16). Each angel performed his duties perfectly, as an intense joy permeated the atmosphere of heaven. It is difficult to imagine that out of this ideal environment would come the world's most ungodly character. Still it happened.

From the writings of Ezekiel, chapter twenty-eight, we learn several matters regarding the original nature, position, and works of Satan. Here is a capsulized summary of these aspects.

1. *His Classification:* He is called a *"cherub"* by Ezekiel (v. 14). This designation is used of an entire classification of angels. They seem to be the highest ranking members of the angelic company.

2. *His Qualities:* In verse twelve we discover that this particular cherub was *"the model of perfection, full of wisdom, and perfect in beauty."* There must have been no other one like him. Among the cherubim he was at the top. These endowments made him the highest creature of God's angelic creation.

3. *His Location:* Ezekiel states that his dwelling was in *"Eden, the garden of God"* (v. 13). This is not, however, the Eden spoken of as the home of

Adam and Eve. Instead, this is a rock garden, laden with precious jewels—ruby, topaz, emerald, chrysolite, onyx, jasper, sapphire, turquoise and beryl. The precise logistics of this site are not critical to the message we are developing.

4. *His Position:* From his first day he was *"anointed"* to serve God as a *"guardian cherub"* (v. 14). The term "anointed" is used of someone who had received a special appointment, especially among men to serve as a prophet, priest or king. The words "Messiah" (Hebrew) and "Christ" (Greek) mean "Anointed One." This indicates, again, the tremendous position he held among the angels.

The term "guardian" seems to suggest that he may have been one of the few angels to actually surround the heavenly throne in its innermost circle. Like the cherubim who were carefully positioned in the most holy place of the Tabernacle, Satan, too, may have formerly served in the direct presence of our Lord (see Exod. 25:20, KJV).

The scene is now set. There is no other angel to match this figure. He is powerful, beautiful and wise. His conduct is flawless. There is nothing for him to gain; he has it all. But something goes wrong, and everything is lost.

The Fall of Satan

God's plans are always perfect. But the ones He

entrusts to fulfill them are sometimes disappointingly imperfect. Satan is one clear example. This angel was of the highest order—a cherub. He was a model angelic being—perfect in all his ways. And then he falls with an irretrievable separation from God. How terrible! Yet how frequently this same episode is repeated in the lives of us humans too. Let's examine this process of alienation, step-by-step.

The various causes for the downfall of Satan are plainly stated in two portions of Scripture—Ezekiel, chapter twenty-eight, and Isaiah, chapter fourteen. Let's explore these passages.

Ezekiel states two chief causes for the transformation of this powerful angel into a wicked foe of God and mankind.

1. *He couldn't handle his massive amount of authority.* While "widespread trade" (Ezek. 28:16) passed through his hands, he couldn't resist the temptation to develop sticky fingers and take some for himself. The old saying that "power tends to corrupt, and absolute power corrupts absolutely" has its roots in Satan. The great authority God gave to him became too much for him to handle.

2. *He couldn't handle his own excellent beauty* (Ezek 28:17). That's pride. He looked at himself, liked what he saw, and became proud. The outcome of this self-inflated diagnosis of himself resulted in poor judgment on his part. His

wisdom, in brief, turned corrupt (v. 17b).

Isaiah also writes about the emergence of Satan from among the good angels. He has a five-point itemization in chapter fourteen of what this insubordinate angel sought to accomplish.

1. *"I will ascend to heaven"* (v. 13a). The beauties of Eden were not enough. He wanted more. Somehow the grass appeared greener in God's yard than in his own.

2. *"I will raise my throne above the stars of God"* (v. 13b). Delegated authority was not enough for this one. He must be number one— the key person at the very top. His ambitious spirit sought for absolute authority. It was fine for others to carry out the laws and orders, but he wanted to make them.

3. *"I will sit enthroned on the mount of the assembly. on the utmost heights of the sacred mountain"* (v. 13c). Ascending above all the other angels wasn't enough. He wanted God's seat as well. This is pride and arrogance at their maximum levels.

4. *"I will ascend above the tops of the clouds"* (v. 14a). Ambition wrongly motivated will result in the pursuit of more of the same. Satan's thirst could not be satisfied. If God's power went up to the clouds, then he would go still higher. Such madness!

5. *"I will make myself like the Most High"* (v. 14b). There are many designations and titles

given to God in the Scriptures, but this one seems to fit best into Satan's schemes. The title "Most High" is first found in Genesis 14:18-19 where it refers to God as the possessor of heaven and earth. Satan wanted it all—from top to bottom.

It was at this absolute point of rebellion that God lowered the boom. He could not tolerate insurrection. Satan had cast aside each of his created privileges in a cheap attempt to selfishly gain more ground. (How this attempt to gain more and more status echoes throughout the human arena too!) He must be judged, along with one-third of the angelic host that accompanied him in his pursuits (Rev. 12:4).

The immediate sentence against this evil company is the revoking of all their former positions and services. The ultimate sentence against them will be an everlasting confinement in the lake of burning brimstone (Rev. 20:7-10). This final judgment will transpire after the millennial reign of Jesus Christ. In the present hour, then, they are still relatively free to continue their campaign of distorting the truth and keeping people from having a personal relationship with our Lord. Much more detail will be presented of this concern in subsequent chapters.

The Name and Titles of Satan

No less than thirty-five ascriptions are given to

this figure in the Bible. He is called many things, and none of them are good. Some of these names picture his authority; others depict his attitude; still others describe his actions. Carefully ponder the detailed charts on the next few pages.

I. NAMES PICTURING SATAN'S AUTHORITY

DESIGNATION	REFERENCE	MEANING
1. Anointed guardian cherub	Ezek. 28:14	He is the highest ranking member of the angelic host.
2. Beelzebub	Mark 3:22	He is lord of the dung pile/king of the flies.
3. Prince of demons	Mark 3:22	He is the commander-in-chief of all fallen angels and demons.
4. Strong man	Luke 11:21	He is the strongest of the fallen angelic beings/stronger than man.
5. Prince of this world	John 12:31; 14:30; 16:11	He is the ruler of each nonbeliever throughout the entire world (1 John 3:8-10).
6. God of this world	2 Cor. 4:4	He is the principal agent behind the formation of the life styles of this world.
7. Prince of the power of the air	Eph. 2:2	He is the ruler of earth's atmosphere and all those who dwell within it ("prince of this world").

II. NAMES PICTURING SATAN'S ATTITUDES

DESIGNATION	REFERENCE	MEANING
1. Satan	Job 1:6-9	He is an adversary—of God Christ, the Holy Spirit, and humans. He is one who hates and resists each of them.
2. Serpent	Gen. 3:15 2 Cor. 11:3 Rev. 12:9	He is a crafty deceiver, full of deadly poison.
3. Enemy/ Adversary	Matt. 13:25, 39 1 Pet. 5:8	He is a constant opponent of the Trinity, the believer and the nonbeliever.
4. Evil one/ Wicked one	Matt. 13:19, 38 1 John 2:13-14; 3:12; 5:18	He is always up to mischief. There is no good in him—none.
5. Wolf/Lion	John 10:12 1 Pet. 5:8	He is vicious, without mercy and powerfully destructive.
6. Belial	2 Cor. 6:15	He is wicked and worthless.
7. Sinner	1 John 3:8	He is forever transgressing God's commandments.

III. NAMES PICTURING SATAN'S ACTIONS

DESIGNATION	REFERENCE	MEANING
1. Devil	Rev. 12:9-10	He is a slanderer—one who attempts to trip another through evil speech.
2. Tempter	Matt. 4:3 1 Thess. 3:5	He is active in enticing people to commit sins.
3. Liar/Father of Lies	John 8:44 Rev. 12:9	He is hopelessly dishonest and deceptive.
4. Murderer	John 8:44	He is not content until each human is dead—spiritually and/or physically.
5. Thief	John 10:10	He is constantly engaged in stealing God's intended blessings from people.
6. Angel of light	2 Cor. 11:14	He is subtle, often disguising himself as an agent from heaven.
7. Dragon	Rev. 12:3; 20:2	He is the leader of the fierce army which opposes Christ and Christianity.

10

The Work of Satan in Heaven

Where is Satan? Is he on the earth attacking spiritual leaders, or is he above the earth commanding his fallen company of evil spirits, or is he in the presence of God attempting to succeed at some diabolical scheme?

The answer from the Scriptures to the question of Satan's dwelling place is threefold: heaven, sky and earth. He is active in each of these areas. Future chapters will deal with his occupations in the sky and earth. In this chapter we will explore his doings in the presence of God.

Satan Accuses Believers

The term "devil" (Greek: *diabolos*, from which we get the words "diabolic" and "diabolical") aptly describes one of his chief activities. This word, in the Greek world of the New Testament, would have been readily understood as "one who accuses another of faults, a slanderer." In three instances this word is even applied to humans who practice releasing poison through the tongue (1 Tim. 3:11; 2 Tim. 3:3; Titus 2:3).

While the devil has been successful in creating a devilish (or accusing) speech among many members of the human species, his primary accusatory labors are waged in heaven itself. John writes, *"The accuser of our brothers [that is, the devil] . . . accuses them before our God day and night"* (Rev. 12:10).

The duration of this satanic activity appears to be ceaseless—"day and night" he slanders Christians. The place for this oratory is also quite clear—"before our God." What remains for us to solve is the reasoning and results behind this fervent exercise of Satan.

1. *The Accusation:* Because Satan is addressed as the "father of lies" (John 8:44), we are inclined to say here that all of his accusations against the believer are totally devoid of truth. But this may not be the case in this instance. Satan does not lie because he is incapable of telling the truth. He lies because it advances his purposes. In the same vein, Satan can, and will, tell the truth if there is any hope of accomplishing his schemes by doing so.

Let's get the setting. Satan appears before God and begins to run through his list of names—Christian names—and to make charges against them. From the data supplied to him from his ambitious cohorts, he senses a large degree of satisfaction in reporting to God the disobedience which is so prevalent among His so-called faithful disciples. There must also be some hope that he will be granted permission to inflict some trial in these believers' lives, as he did in the case of Job (see Job 1-2).

The Father, then, listens to Satan's parade of assaults. The ball, so to speak, is now in His court. He must act upon these reports. How He does so is seen in the following point.

2. *The Attorney:* When Satan approaches God the Father with his detailed list of complaints, a court scene in heaven is created (see the diagram on the following page). The Father is the Judge; the devil is the prosecuting attorney; and Jesus is the believer's defendant. This is what John probably had in mind when he said, "*I write this to you so that you will not sin. But if anybody does sin, we have one who speaks to the Father in our defense—Jesus Christ, the Righteous One*" (1 John 2:1).

When we sin, one of the devil's workers takes down a note of the offense and sends it along to Satan himself. He, in turn, reports the matter to the Father, in hopes of gaining some action against this believer. The Father, then, turns to

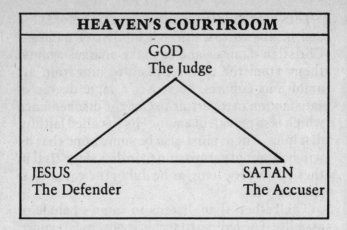

HEAVEN'S COURTROOM

GOD
The Judge

JESUS
The Defender

SATAN
The Accuser

Jesus and inquires about the accuracy of the accusation. Jesus is left with two possible responses.

First, if the believer has repented of his sin before the time Satan makes his presentation, then Jesus proudly announces that there is no record of any such matter against this Christian. Through the believer's repentance, his sins have been washed away in the blood of Jesus (1 John 1:7; Rev. 12:10-11). In this case the Father overrides Satan's charges, pronounces the accused person innocent, and throws the whole deal out of court!

Praise the Lord for this triumph over Satan! But there is another side to this story too.

Second, if the believer has not repented by the time Satan makes his presentation before the Father, then Jesus is left to confirm the accusation. The believer is guilty as charged. There can be no defense against the truth. The Father is then compelled to render justice in the matter. When people sin—including Christians—they must face the consequences. God seems to satisfy Satan's appetite, for the moment, as a sentence of chastisement is rendered against the unrepentant Christian (see Heb. 12).

By going one step farther into this scene we may find another positive note. While Satan shouts for glee over his apparent victory in heaven's court, little does he realize that God will use this sentencing to refine His own disciples (see 1 Cor. 5:5, 11:27-34; Heb. 12)! In the end, Satan has lost again.

Overcoming Satan

From the same pericope of Scripture that tells us of Satan's accusations, we also learn of the believer's threefold defense against him (Rev. 12:10-11). John writes that *they overcame him (the devil) by:*

1. *the blood of the Lamb*
2. *the word of their testimony*
3. *not loving their lives so much as to shrink from death.*

The first of these three items has already been discussed. By confessing our sins, and having them removed through the blood of Jesus, our Lord can thereby defend us against Satan. Living in a constant attitude of readiness to repent the instant we sin is a strong cure for potential chastisement.

The second piece of artillery we can effectively launch against Satan is a verbal confession of Jesus as our Lord. Some believers prefer to be "silent witnesses." But the Bible knows no such disciples (see John 12:42-43). The victory of Christ in a believer's life is always best seen among those who testify openly and unashamedly.

The third weapon we can use against the devil is self-denial. The more we are involved in securing the well-being of others, the less Satan will be able to tackle and cripple us. Those Christians who have learned to practice their love fervently have also found a way of overcoming Satan.

Stated simply, the best defense against Satan is a strong offense with Jesus Christ!

11

The Work of Satan in the Sky

In chapter three we learned that God's angels are quite active in our atmosphere. Here we will discover that Satan, too, is busy in this realm.

Satanic Wars

Satan is boldly opposed to God's plans. That means he must also be in constant confrontation with God's angelic hosts. Satan's war with God is not so much a direct combat situation as it is an indirect one. The devil utilizes his weapons in attacking angels and people. (See the chart on the following page.)

When Daniel prayed for insight so that he might understand the revelation God had given to him, his request was answered in heaven

SATAN IS A FOURFOLD ENEMY

1. ENEMY OF JESUS	2. ENEMY OF ANGELS	3. ENEMY OF BELIEVERS	4. ENEMY OF NONBELIEVERS
Matt. 4:1-10; 12:22-30 Mark 1:13; 4:15 Luke 4:1-2; 22:3-4 John 13:27	Dan. 10:13-11:1 Jude 9 Rev. 12:7-12	Luke 13:16; 22:31 Acts 5:3 Rom. 16:20 1 Cor. 5:5; 7:5 2 Cor. 2:11; 11:3,14 1 Thess. 2:18 1 Tim. 1:20; 5:15 Rev. 2:9, 13, 24; 3:9; 12:9	Matt. 13:4, 19 Mark 4:15 Acts 26:18 2 Cor. 4:3-4 2 Thess. 2:9-10 Rev. 20:7

immediately. But Daniel had to wait for twenty-one days before he personally received God's reply. Why the delay? Because God's angels were prevented by Satan's army from getting through any sooner! Read it for yourself in Daniel, chapter ten.

Moses was informed by the Lord that he would not see the Promised Land. His ministry would only take the tiny nation of Israel to the doorway of Canaan. So Moses died in the wilderness. But after his death it was the archangel Michael who had to dispute "*with the devil about the body of Moses*" (Jude 9).

Jude apparently gathered his data here from a noncanonical book entitled, *The Assumption of Moses*. In this account of Moses' funeral it is stated that Michael is commissioned to bury the body of this great patriarch. Satan, on the other hand, opposed this action on two grounds: (1) He asserted supremacy in the matter and claimed that the body, therefore, belonged to him; (2) He accused Moses of committing murder, making him one of his own disciples. The attempt on Satan's part, however, availed nothing. Still, the episode provides us with another glimpse of how Satan wages conflicts in the sky.

Another illustration comes to us, not from the past, but from the future. In a prophecy revealed to John, he is told of a time when Satan and all of his assistants will engage in the hottest battle ever experienced by them and God's angels. The actual period of this hostility will occur three-and-a-half years prior to Christ's second coming (see Rev. 12). At that time the heavens will be greatly shaken. Not a single member of Satan's army will escape this crushing defeat.

Once Satan is cast out of the skies and onto the earth, he will work with unparalleled haste and anger. He knows this defeat will soon be followed by a far more serious and permanent one. So he confronts men swiftly and bitterly. In forty-two months, however, it will be all over. The godly angels will round up these evil spirits and cast them into the abyss (see Rev. 12:13-17, 20:1-6).

The lid on the abyss is not sealed forever, however. Attached to it is a one thousand-year timer. After one millennium these evil forces will again be released to work among the nations. For a short time they will scurry among the nations in order that they might present one final offensive against God. But the attempt is doomed from the start. Again, they will be captured by God's angels. This time they will be sentenced to spend forever and ever in the lake of burning sulphur (Rev. 20:1-3; 7-10). See the diagram on the following page for details.

Satanic Weather

In a previous chapter it was shown that God's angels can directly influence weather conditions

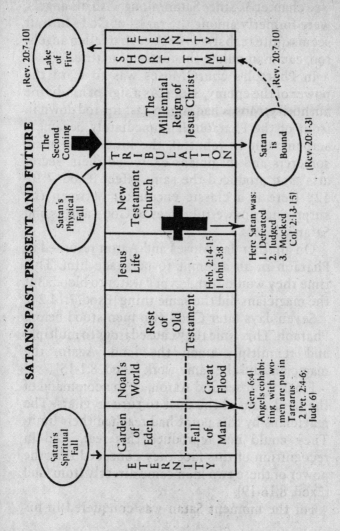

SATAN'S PAST, PRESENT AND FUTURE

					The Second Coming		

Satan's Spiritual Fall

Satan's Physical Fall

Lake of Fire (Rev. 20:7-10)

Garden of Eden	Noah's World	Rest of Old Testament	Jesus' Life	New Testament Church	T R I B U L A T I O N	The Millennial Reign of Jesus Christ	S H O R T T I M E

E T E R N I T Y

E T E R N I T Y

Fall of Man

Great Flood

Gen. 6:4
Angels cohabitting with women are put in Tartarus - 2 Pet. 2:4-6; Jude 6)

Heb. 2:14-15
1 John 3:8

Here Satan was:
1. Defeated
2. Judged
3. Mocked
Col. 2:13-15)

Satan is Bound (Rev. 20:1-3)

(Rev. 20:7-10)

95

(see chapter 3). Since Satan, along with his angels, were formerly among the ranks of God's host, it seems quite realistic to declare that fallen angels, too, can manipulate the forces of nature.

In Pharaoh's court Moses was to learn the power of the enemy, Satan. As a sign of his divine authority, Moses had Aaron cast his rod down in front of the Pharaoh. It immediately became a serpent. But in rebuttal, the king's wise men, sorcerers and magicians exercised their "secret arts" and produced the same effect (Exod. 7:10-12)! Here is a classic encounter between the surprisingly powerful forces of God's angels and Satan's angels.

On another day Moses and Aaron returned to Pharaoh in an attempt to persuade him. This time they would turn Egypt's water to blood. But the magicians did the same thing (Exod. 7:14-24).

Seven days later God's two men stood before Pharaoh. This time they caused frogs to multiply and remultiply upon the land. Again, the magicians did the same work (Exod. 8:1-15).

Finally, Moses and Aaron, at the command of the Lord, caused the dust to turn to gnats. The magicians by this point had reached their limit. They could not reproduce this feat. And in recognition of this fact they conceded that the power of these two men came directly from God (Exod. 8:16-19).

For the moment Satan was conquered in his

schemes. But the revelation of his powers in this conflict must serve to dispel any notion we might possess concerning his weakness to effect changes in the course of nature.

It may well be that certain natural phenomena (such as storms—see Mark 4:35-41) have a satanic base. We mustn't be afraid to challenge these destructive forces in Jesus' name, for through God's angels a miraculous tranquility can come. Reports of a changed course in a tornado's (and similar storm's) path because of prayer are not at all uncommon. Naturally, this does not suggest that Christians can manipulate the weather by whispering a prayer. But it does encourage us to recognize the possible demonic nature of certain storms and to resist them, just as our Lord did.

12

The Work of Satan in the Church

It should be no surprise that Satan's chief operations are waged against Christ's disciples and the local church (where these converts are to be strengthened and trained). Satan knows all too well that if he can curb the effectiveness of the church, then all of God's kingdom is hindered. So Sunday after Sunday the devil goes to church so that he might prevent God's plans from succeeding.

There is no doubt over Satan's triumphs in the church at the local and hierarchical levels. He has made a wide and well-paved path for himself here. Let's consider the strategies of this foe as he endeavors to crush Christ's Church.

Deception Through Light

When Satan attacks light, he often uses light as his primary weapon. In other words, the best way to work in the Church is to enter through the door marked "subtleness." Satan is crafty and shrewd. He recognizes that an open and clear-cut denial of God's truths would be rejected in most circles. So he maintains a margin of spiritual truths, while mixing them with subtle errors.

Some of the chief errors (or lies) in Satan's operation within the Church are these: (1) the fallibility of the Scriptures; (2) the supremacy of experience over scriptural authority; (3) the addition of extra-biblical data; (4) the multiplied legalistic demands for salvation; (5) the liberal notion that because God is love there can never be any hell; (6) the out-of-balance emphasis on spiritual gifts as a sign of conversion; and (7) the rejection of a literal devil. There are many others that could be added to this list, but this compilation is highly suggestive.

The underlying theme of each satanic attack upon the local church is spelled D-E-C-E-P-T-I-O-N. The trick is this—get religious people to believe religious-sounding material that is only half-true. If you can do this, especially in vital areas, then you can often keep people from effective service and maybe even from heaven itself!

Paul informed the Corinthians of this ever-present danger when he said, "*I am afraid that just as Eve was deceived by the serpent's cunning, your minds may somehow be led astray from your sincere and pure devotion to Christ"* (2 Cor. 11:3). The threat to the church was real. Paul's concern is not impractical. Satan will attack the sanctity of the Christian assembly.

It isn't difficult to understand why Satan works diligently with pastors in his offensive against the local church. If he can control the shepherds, then he can sway a large portion of the sheep. If this one key position can be dominated by the subtle combination of truth and error, then those who yield themselves to this leader's ministry will fall prey to the same snare.

Paul writes about these fallen church officials, and he says they are *"false apostles, deceitful workmen, masquerading as apostles of Christ. And no wonder, for Satan himself masquerades as an angel of light. It is not surprising, then, if his servants masquerade as servants of righteousness"* (2 Cor. 11:13-15; cf. 1 Tim. 4:1; Rev. 2:9).

In nations of light, Satan works through so-called "Christians" (John 13:2, 21-30). Error does *not* mean the opposite of truth; instead, it refers to any degree of deviation from the truth—no matter how slight or subtle. In America Satan is working from behind the pulpit, on the church board, and in the pew to cause the church to lose its freshness, its sharpness, and its full functioning power. He is at work to make people good, but not spiritual; to make people smart, but not edified;

to keep people busy, but not doing what God wants accomplished! Ignorance of these points will permit the "angel of light" and his "servants" to manipulate our churches as though everything were fine, when, in fact, the real condition, from God's perspective, is weakness, aimlessness and fruitlessness.

The cure for this ignorance is spiritual education. The systematic, topical and expository *teaching* of the Scriptures is indispensable in the process of Christian maturity. No genuine Bible study equals no spiritual growth. I must be emphatic in this point. Much so-called Bible study is, in effect, a pooling of opinions and feelings or the placing of a pound of emphasis upon a mere ounce of truth (or the reverse; the placing of an ounce of emphasis on a pound of truth). This is not the Lord's idea of genuine Bible study. The roles of a *prepared teacher* and an *eager student* are imperative in the successful church that defeats Satan and expands God's kingdom.

It should be the standard procedure of each Christian to evaluate the pastor(s) who are over him in the Lord. You mustn't submit to men who freely mix personal interpretations with scriptural doctrines. Truth and error don't combine. If the Word of God is not the measurement for all truth or the final pattern for all faith and practice, then it's time you move! Go to a church that both preaches and practices the Word of God. It is the only way you can be protected against error, as well as the only way you can be productive for Christ.

Premature Ambition

Another of the subtle traps created by Satan for the destruction of the church's effectiveness is the premature placement of someone into a leadership role. We each so desperately want all believers to serve Christ through His church that sometimes we enlist people before they are ready for the position offered to them.

Here's a story that really hurts. When I completed my second year of college, I met Christ as my personal Lord and Savior. Within a few weeks of this marvelous experience I was rehearsing with three other Christians who wanted to start a singing group. It was thrilling. Three months passed and I found myself teaching an adult Bible class. Nine months after this I was hired as assistant pastor. Another three months went along (at this point it was sixteen months after my conversion) and I was hired to be a full-time pastor, while finishing my college degree!

Naturally, I was excited at all of these advancements. The Lord, I thought, surely was going to use me. I loved pastoring. Church attendance rose; people were coming to the altar often; and everything seemed to be just perfect. Then something happened. Someone told me my job was to *teach* the Bible, not merely talk about it. I was shocked. Then I remembered how one of my parishioners had invited me over to explain to him the difference between a gap eschatology and a parenthetical ecclesiology, as that difference related to the abomination of desolation! I could barely find the book of Matthew (and I had been pastoring for nearly a year!). But this layman could turn with ease to Daniel, Zechariah, 2 Thessalonians, and so forth. Oh, was I ever embarrassed.

This shallowness haunted me. I began to read commentaries, buy theology books, and ask some serious questions. By the time I realized I hadn't been doing my job as a pastor, the people were beginning to get upset. They liked me the way I was *before* I discovered my responsibility was to be a teacher of the Word of God. They liked my stories and jokes (all in the name of Jesus, of course). I had them laughing or crying all the time, *but no one was really growing up. I had a position for which I was not prepared, and, worse yet, the congregation enjoyed it best when I was at my worst as a teacher.* This tragedy is not uncommon, I have since discovered. Many pastors are prematurely poised behind a pulpit without any real sense of what they are there to accomplish (some never get out of this stage!).

I have known churches to carry this "art" of getting people involved to such an extreme position that the nonactive members are called upon to serve in some capacity with the idea that this job will magically turn them into active and spiritual people. The fruit from this manipulating, however, is usually counter-productive. This just isn't God's method.

Paul warned of the danger of misplacing the believer by stating that this worker might *"become conceited and fall under the same judgment as the devil . . . and into the devil's trap"* (1 Tim. 3:6-7).

Young believers or new converts, as precious and ambitious as they might be, are not God's choice for leadership positions in the church. Let them work patiently. Their hour will arrive. And when it does come, they will be even better equipped to manage the tasks at hand than if they had jumped in earlier. Today's overemphasis upon the youth and the Church of *tomorrow* has practically neglected God's sound principles of management for the Church of *today*.

In the same vein, it can (and must!) be plainly pronounced that premature ambition finds its prey among some older church members too. It is a fine thing to care for each detail of the church's operation, but sometimes it is the people who do not possess leadership gifts who want to place their palms on the big wheel of the church controls. Frankly, the failure on the part of the church to stop these misguided persons has caused unimaginable damage to the church's productivity!

There is an imperative principle here: *Discern who are the gifted leaders in your assembly (there may be only several); then, give them the authority to lead. Let the rest joyfully follow in their spiritual steps!* If anyone cannot submit to this truth, then he needs some serious counseling. (See Rom. 12:5-8; 1 Cor. 12:28; and Eph. 4:11 for these leadership gifts.)

Remember this passage: *"Obey your [spiritual] leaders and submit to their authority. They keep watch over you as men who must give an account. Obey them so their work will be a joy, not a burden, for that would be of no advantage to you"* (Heb. 13:17).

An Unteachable Attitude

In this point is a truth that many of us have yet to adequately recognize. It is dangerous to be unteachable or stubborn. Yet many Christians are bent on holding on to their critical spirits.

It seems we have to think we know something, that we're as smart as most of those around us. We don't want to be corrected. We don't like to change. We want to stay the way we are. And with that attitude we assuredly will remain the same!

How unfortunate it is that these persons do not realize they have, by their self-erected attitudes, bound themselves to the will of Satan. They have become pawns in his hand. How tragic is the fate of a self-governed person, a self-made person, an unteachable person.

Notice Paul's comments: *"Those who oppose him [the Lord's servant] he must gently instruct, in the hope that God will grant them repentance leading them to a knowledge of the truth, and that they will come to their senses and escape from the trap of the devil, who has taken them captive to do his will"* (2 Tim. 2:25-26).

Anyone who stubbornly refuses to follow the godly counsel of another Christian (the context above happens to indicate a church leader), then he automatically becomes the devil's puppet! How often I have seen this happen. In each church with which I have had any association it wasn't long before it became apparent that a few persons (and sometimes a great many more than a few) are irreversibly bent (and usually unconsciously bent) on opposing God's will. The spirit of submission and humility could not be found in these persons' hearts. They were in Satan's grasp. My only prayer was that I might maintain a gentle spirit toward them and that they might come to their senses and repent.

Every church has members like this. They must be recognized. And their destructive influence must be seen as being satanic. Sometimes prayer, patience and love will win them over. But other times, the course taken may require confrontation, exhortation, rebuke and possibly even excommunication (see Matt. 18:15-18; 2 Cor. 5:1-13;

1 Tim. 1:18-20; Titus 3:9-11).

Persecution

Satan's charge against the Church is not only internal. It is also external as well. Jesus told the church at Smyrna these insightful words: *"Do not be afraid of what you are about to suffer. I tell you, the devil will put some of you in prison to test you, and you will suffer persecution for ten days. Be faithful, even to the point of death, and I will give you the crown of life"* (Rev. 2:10).

Here is a prophecy and a promise. The former is sad news; the latter is satisfying news. Jesus told this church that some of its members would be imprisoned, persecuted and even put to death. (This isn't the kind of prophecy that very many persons would even accept today as being of the Lord. Maybe we need to widen our knowledge of God's will. See 1 Peter 4:1-2, 19, for instance.) At the same time, Jesus informed them of the reward that would await these faithful martyrs.

Churches are not exempt from serious problems. How little we understand this statement as Americans. Our land is free, and our worship is without any political harassment. But this condition is not to be found in many of the world's 210 countries. In most Moslem and Communist countries, for instance, it is even against the law to import a single Bible, or to witness in Jesus' name! Countless tens of thousands have been slaughtered indiscriminately in these satanically governed countries. Some of the facts available to us on the persecution of people (including Christians) in various countries are too horrible to imagine.

A casual glance at any book on Church history will open our eyes too. Persecution is no stranger to the Church of Jesus Christ. Our Lord suffered, and so will His Church. You can count on it.

Conclusion

Jesus seeks to be the Lord of the local church, but so does Satan. Both want their wills to be accomplished. We must discern Satan's strategies and oppose him. We must make Christ the focal point of our church.

When Jesus designed the Church, He fortified it in such a way that even the gates of hell couldn't prevail against it (Matt. 16:18). His Church was designed for victory. He equipped His Church with armor. He provided a manual of instructions to serve as a guide to this victory. If we will follow His instructions, the results are guaranteed!

13

The Work of Satan with the Believer

Among the various activities of Satan, no other matter receives more attention in the Scriptures than his combat with believers. It is safe to conclude, from the testimony of the Bible, that the devil's number one occupation is to undermine, hinder, and thwart Christians from making spiritual advancements and from rendering spiritual service. A casual look at our churches, communities, nation and world will quickly confirm this astonishing statement.

Satan utilizes any number of devices to debilitate or destroy his victims. No less than seven weapons in the devil's arsenal are discussed in the Scriptures. We will consider these in this chapter, remembering that we should not, in Paul's words, be *unaware of his schemes* (2 Cor. 2:11). It is through an awareness of these diabolic techniques that we can spot his involvement and cast him out of the way.

1. Ignorance of Scripture

If the devil can be successful in keeping a person out of the Scriptures, then he can instantly remove any hope for this person's spiritual development. The Word of God is the believer's nutrition. Each believer, *"like newborn babies [is to] crave pure spiritual milk [from the Scriptures], so that by it [he] may grow up in [his] salvation"* (1 Pet. 2:2). A lack of understanding in the message of the Bible will culminate in a corresponding spiritual deficiency.

Jesus said, *"When anyone hears the message about the kingdom and does not understand it, the evil one [that is, Satan] comes and snatches away what was sown in his heart"* (Matt. 13:19). The context makes it plain that Jesus is discussing here the condition of an unbeliever. But the principle on the activity of Satan remains unchanged when carried over to the Christian circle. Satan works no less ambitiously to "snatch away" the Word from the believer's heart too.

If Satan can keep you from Bible studies, then he will have succeeded in keeping you from a major part of God's plans for your life. Resist the temptation to stay home, and go to a Bible study with other believers.

Additionally, get in the Word by yourself. Read the Scriptures regularly. Read with penetration. Read with application. Read your Bible, learn God's ways and defeat the devil. You are what you read.

2. Distortion of Scripture

Here is a subtle twist on the above point. If Satan can keep you from the Word of God, he is well pleased. But if he can interest you in a distorted interpretation of the Scriptures, then he is no less satisfied. The perversion of knowledge, as well as the absence of it, is no less devastating for spiritual growth.

The classic illustrations of satanic distortion of God's Word are found in the first book of each testament. In Genesis the devil tells Eve, in opposition to God's previous statements, *"You will not surely die. . . . For God knows that when you eat of it your eyes will be opened, and you will be like God, knowing good and evil"* (Gen. 3:4-5). That's a lie, a distortion of what God actually said. Nevertheless, both Adam and Eve swallowed the bait and were keenly disappointed as a result of following Satan's advice.

In Matthew we read of how Satan tempted Jesus through the use of the Old Testament Scriptures (Matt. 4:1-11). The devil can quote Scripture. But his use of the Word is always a trick to alienate us from God's truth and will.

Today, there are multitudes of professing Christians who denounce the accuracy of the Bible. For them the Scriptures are only inspired here and there. And, as one might expect, they alone are capable of ascertaining the precise spots that are supposedly inspired. This approach to the Word of God is called "liberalism." Some prefer to call it modern scholarship, but in the end the result is the same—distortion of the Scriptures by listening to Satan's lies.

Many churches, including complete denominations, reject the notion that the Scriptures are genuinely inspired by God. Most seminaries—from which we derive the bulk of the nation's pastors—do *not* teach that the Bible is the final authority for doctrine and conduct! This may sound astonishing to you, but it is, nevertheless, quite true. It is possible that your pastor was never even required to take a single course in a careful examination of a Bible book. If this is the case, he isn't alone.

While over 90 percent of America's women, according to a recent survey, believe in God, less than 10 percent of these same women accept the Bible's inspiration! Surely this is clear proof of Satan's success in attacking the whole counsel of the Bible.

3. Marital Problems

It is no secret that the home has become the

primary concern of the Church in recent years. Christian families are experiencing a devastating crisis throughout America. The divorce rate among believers is shockingly high. We must find the answer to why this is the case.

There may be a rather broad diversity of causes for marital maladjustments (such as finances, health, in-laws, children, different backgrounds and values, etc.), but one factor that cannot be overlooked is satanic involvement. We mustn't assume that the devil is only involved in "spiritual" matters. He also frequently attempts to destroy marriages between believers.

Many Christian counselors are revealing through their literature today that a large percentage of their workload entails marital counseling. Further, they make it unmistakably plain that very many of these problems stem from sexual difficulties. Here is an almost certain fact: If the husband or wife cannot enjoy their bed partnership, then their whole marriage is in danger. This statement is *not* an oversimplification.

God is astutely aware of this situation. Since He gave to each of us a sexual attraction for our mates, it is important for us to recognize and fulfill this aspect of our creation-design in accordance with God's plans. Notice Paul's solemn advice in this regard.

Since there is so much immorality, each man should have his own wife, and each woman her own husband. The husband should fulfill his marital duty to his wife, and likewise the wife to her husband. The wife's body does not belong to her alone but also to her husband. In the same way, the husband's body does not belong to him alone but also to his wife. Do not deprive each other except by mutual consent and for a time, so that you may devote yourselves to prayer. Then come together again so that Satan will not tempt you because of your lack of self-control. (1 Cor. 7:2-5)

A husband's body belongs to his wife; and a wife's body belongs to her husband. There is only one authorized release from the bed partnership (and even this is temporary)—to pray in separate rooms during the night (and this must be by mutual consent). Otherwise Satan will put a sexual wedge between a couple. God made mates so that they would enjoy one another's bodies.

Guard yourself at this juncture. And if you feel a need for assistance, don't be afraid to talk with a Christian pastor. He has heard concerns in this area before. It won't be new to him. He can help you. Take the time to go and get help, before it gets out of hand altogether (but don't assume it is totally out of control until you obtain professional assistance). If your mate won't join you, then go alone. But by all means go!

Also, you could be tremendously enriched by visiting your local Christian bookstore and purchasing several books on this vital subject. Tim and Beverly LaHaye's book, *The Act of Marriage*, is an excellent tool. And there are others. Check them over carefully, then buy the ones best suited for your particular case.

4. Unforgiveness

Here is a powerful Scripture that should not be forgotten:

Now instead, you ought to forgive and comfort him [a former church member who was found guilty of sexual immorality], so that he will not be overwhelmed by excessive sorrow. I urge you, therefore, to reaffirm your love for him. The reason I wrote you was to see if you would stand the test and be obedient in everything. If you forgive anyone, I also forgive him. And what I have forgiven—if there was anything to forgive— I have forgiven in the sight of Christ for your sake, in order that Satan might not outwit us. For we are not unaware of his schemes. (2 Cor. 2:7-11)

Paul is talking here about a man, who a year

earlier, had been found guilty of sexual immorality. (His story can be found in 1 Corinthians 5:1-13; read it carefully.) This man was excommunicated from the church (or, as the Scriptures state it, delivered *"unto Satan for the destruction of the flesh"*). But since excommunication is never intended to be a permanent arrangement, the prayer was that this guilty man would repent so that he might be ultimately restored to the fellowship of the church.

Paul is telling the Corinthian Christians that because this man repented, they must now receive him back without any unforgiveness in their hearts. Why? Because God had forgiven him. And when God forgives, we, too, must forgive. Whenever a believer harbors unforgiveness (or negative/critical feelings in his heart) toward someone whom God has forgiven, then he opens a door for satanic attack. We must be a forgiving people, or we will be a spiritually weak people.

So many Christians and churches have lost their cutting edge by allowing Satan a foothold in their relationships with one another. There is only one cure for this ailment—restoration through repentance. Confrontation, apology and forgiveness must never be allowed to take a back seat in our dealings with other people—saved or lost.

This advice does not mean we offer a blanket

forgiveness to everyone, regardless of their action. Never. All of this does mean, however, that whenever people make a move toward repentance, we must make an equal move in the direction of forgiveness (see Luke 17:1-3).

I am very familiar with a church in Ohio that experienced the greatest revival of its history when it began to apply this truth. And I really do mean *revival*. The pastor couldn't even preach in a number of the services. People would rise, go to the microphone, and confess their lack of faithfulness to that local body. It was fantastic. Homes were reunited, broken relationships were mended, and Christ was honored. The spirit of forgiveness was so intense that often a regular one-hour service would be turned into a three or four-hour meeting. There were testimonies and praises one after another, as people waited in long lines to share what God was doing in their hearts. Revival is, doubtlessly, one of the prime needs in most of our churches.

5. Your Thought Life

If Satan can conquer your thoughts, then he has the rest of you as well. It is this central member of the body—our minds—which the devil most often attacks.

To a very large extent, our spirituality is determined by our mind. We are only as spiritual or mature as our thoughts. Solomon states it in this manner: "For as [a person] thinketh in his heart, so is he" (Prov. 23:7 KJV). We are, in effect, the sum of our thought life—nothing more, nothing less and nothing else.

Your mind is the chief organ God uses to enrich your walk with Him (see Rom. 12:1-2; Eph. 4:17-24; Col. 3:1-10). It is also Satan's primary target.

Paul writes, "I am afraid that just as Eve was deceived by the serpent's cunning, your minds may somehow be led astray" (2 Cor. 11:3).

Again, Paul says, "For though we live in the world, we do not wage war as the world does. The weapons we fight with are not the weapons of the world. On the contrary, they have divine power to demolish [satanic] strongholds. We demolish arguments and every pretension that sets itself up against the knowledge of God, and we take captive every thought to make it obedient to Christ" (2 Cor. 10:3-5).

The gist of these two verses spells out one inevitable fact—Christians will have to learn how to combat the thoughts that do not serve to accomplish God's will. This, naturally, entails far more than simply fighting Christ-rejecting thoughts. It includes resting every negative/critical mood (Phil. 4:7-10), each worry and doubt (Isa. 26:3; 1 Pet. 5:7-8; Heb. 11:6), and all careless nonsense (Matt. 12:36-37; Eph. 5:4-21)!

Several years ago I taught a course on

Satanology. Each time I approach this topic I can sense a real resistance developing. It is clear that Satan doesn't want to be exposed through a teaching that is specifically designed to defeat him.

One morning as I sat at the breakfast table several negative thoughts crossed my mind. I more or less ignored them. Soon there were more critical thoughts—this time about the pathetic state of so many evangelical churches. Following this came thoughts of anger. And finally, I found myself furious with God's methods in dealing with this world and His Church.

My body was relaxed, and my face showed no signs of hostility, but inside my thoughts were teeming with utter disgust. My mind even told me to hate God for His stupid management of the universe. I couldn't believe this was happening. The ultimate negative thought was murder—I wanted, in my mind, to actually kill God!

With that final harassment I went to my knees and asked to be forgiven for these incredible thoughts. I wanted my mind to be released and cleansed. Next, I told Satan to leave my mind alone, and that I was reserving it exclusively for the Lordship of Jesus Christ. Instantly the attack ceased. I felt such a relief that I wanted to cry with praise. My thoughts made a 180 degrees turnabout in only seconds!

Since this experience, I have sought to screen my thoughts very carefully. When critical thoughts enter my mind now, I give them over to Christ right away. There is no room for the mind of Satan when Christ's thoughts are in control.

Whenever your thoughts cannot bow their knee in obedience to the glory of Christ, then they ought to be expelled. Obviously, you cannot always prevent an initial thought or two of disobedience from entering your mind, but shortly after their introduction you should stand prepared to kill these thoughts in their tracks, and then to remove them through the power of prayer from your mind. Ask God for His assistance. He is willing to help you clean up your mind.

The best overall defense against satanic thoughts is to have a strong and active relationship with Christ and His Church. Busy hands in the Lord's work will repel many would-be dangerous thoughts (see Prov. 3:5-6, 16:3 KJV; Rom. 12:1-2; Eph. 4:17-24). Remember Ananias and Saphira (Acts 5:1-11).

A complete separate volume could be devoted to this single topic of satanic involvement. Some fine teaching in this vein may be found in Watchman Nee's book, *The Spiritual Man*.

6. Lukewarmness

There is nothing that satisfies the devil quite

like a lukewarm relationship between a believer and Christ. Why is this so? Because no one can hinder the works of Christ so greatly as the person who feels he is "okay," when in fact he is *"wretched, pitiful, poor, blind and naked"* (Rev. 3:14-22).

You can't tell a lukewarm person to do more; he thinks he is already doing enough, maybe even more than his share. You can't tell a lukewarm person anything new; he already knows all he needs to know about the things that really matter. And you can't tell a lukewarm person to change; he sees no advantage in alterations of the established traditional patterns.

Jesus said, *"The thief [the devil] comes only to steal and kill and destroy; I have come that they may have life, and have it to the full"* (John 10:10). The archenemy of your life seeks to make your walk with the Lord a dull one, unappealing and burdensome. He will remove its sterling qualities, if he can. Don't allow him this opportunity.

7. Any Unconfessed Sin

James has given us these practical words: *"Submit yourselves, then, to God. Resist the devil, and he will flee from you. Come near to God and he will come near to you. Wash your hands, you sinners, and purify your hearts, you double-minded. Grieve, mourn and wail. Change your laughter to mourning and your joy to gloom.*

Humble yourselves before the Lord, and he will lift you up" (James 4:7-10).

Sin can be a monstrous thing. How lightly we sometimes treat it. But James says to weep, to howl, to stop laughing and to become sorrowful. Anything can be done too extremely and become harmful, but of late we have no reason to fear we are cracking down on sin with too heavy a stick. If anything we have been far too light in our treatment of sin—at home, in our churches, on our jobs, and in our government (at all levels).

There is a practical observation many have made about the nature of sin. It goes something like this: the longer you put off repentance, the harder it becomes to deal with it.

Don't delay your repentance. The instant after you sin, repent. Tell God you're sorry. Ask for forgiveness immediately. Waiting only prolongs and multiplies the agony. Confess it right away. Lift a silent prayer wherever you are and get rid of the matter once and for all! Don't give Satan a chance to knock you down.

It isn't difficult to defeat Satan, since he is actually already defeated (Heb. 2:14-15; 1 John 3:8, 4:4; James 4:7). The Christian life isn't difficult either (Matt. 11:28-30; 1 John 5:3-4). If we are humbly feeding on the things of God, and if we are genuinely feeding others to the best of our ability, then the path of personal victory is beneath our feet, and our walk is secure!

14

The Work of Satan with the Unbeliever

In the final analysis there are only two sets of people on this earth. One group belongs to God. The other group belongs to Satan. The short of it cannot be stated any more clearly than these choice words from John's pen:

"No one who is born of God will continue to sin. . . . because he has been born of God. This is how we know who the children of God are and who the children of the devil are: Anyone who does not do what is right is not a child of God" (1 John 3:9-10).

You and I are classified by God as being either one of His children or a child of Satan. There is no other alternative as far as God is concerned. Those who love Christ and gladly receive His orders are His own. And those who do not make this same submission are, without an exception, receiving their orders from Satan (whether they are conscious of this relationship or not).

Let's look now at the influence the devil exerts upon those who have not become Christians.

Spiritual Blindness

The number one operation of Satan with the unbeliever is to keep him in a perpetual state of spiritual blindness to the pure truth. He does this through a sixfold program: (1) liberalism, (2) cultism; (3) occultism; (4) agnosticism; (5) atheism; and (6) world religions. Each of these points requires individual attention.

1. *Liberalism:* There are many shades to this first member of the satanic army, but the one underlying element in each phase is religious deception. In the Western world this is Satan's most lethal spiritual bomb. On the surface it appears innocent enough. But when all the colors are shown, its devastating effects become apparent.

Liberalism is pseudo-Christianity. In other words, it is a unique attempt to be Christian, while at the same time to be found faithful to major or minor points in other religions. Liberalism also holds the discoveries of the modern sciences at least one step above the revelation of the Bible. In effect, truth, for the liberal, is subjective, relative, subject to change and largely yet undiscovered.

The guidepost for liberalism is twentieth-century education. The human brain, philosophical logic, and computerized, scientific proofs are actually the "gods" of liberalism.

For the liberal it is only those segments of the Scriptures which can be presently proven that are accepted as truth. Naturally, this approach has little room for the inclusion of the miraculous.

This satanic brew of half God and half man's ideas is the most popular of all the devil's works. It is a subtle attempt to combine the so-called best of the Bible with the best of the sciences. The mixture, however, always fails to include certain indispensable cardinal doctrines of the true Christian faith (such as the inspiration of the Scriptures, the deity of Christ, the need for personal salvation through Jesus Christ, the spiritual depravity of man as being his greatest weakness, the condemnation of the unbeliever, and the reality of an everlasting hell and heaven).

Liberalism is unquestionably a system of religious thought that comes from deceiving spirits. Notice the chart on the following page.

2. *Cultism:* The term "cult," itself, does not possess any judgmental meaning. It simply refers

CONTRASTING THE BIBLE WITH LIBERALISM

THE BIBLICAL RECORD	LIBERAL BELIEFS
1. Bible's inspiration	1. Bible's errors
2. Bible's authority	2. Scientific proofs
3. Divine creation	3. Evolution
4. Jesus is Savior	4. Jesus is example
5. Jesus' substitutionary atonement	5. Man's good works
6. Resurrection of Christ	6. Resurrection of Christ's ideas
7. Balance of God's love and wrath	7. God only loves
8. God is Father of Christians	8. God is Father of world
9. People are sinful	9. People make mistakes and/or are sick
10. Heaven and hell are real	10. Heaven might be real Hell is on this earth

128

to any religious group which deviates in some way from the more customary body of beliefs held by the majority. As such, in America, a cult would be any religious body which significantly departs from "traditional" Christianity. That's a pretty broad definition, but it will serve our general purposes.

Walter R. Martin, in his exceptional book, *The Kingdom of the Cults*, adds this note to our definition. He believes that a cult is a religious body which has gathered around a specific person or person's interpretation of the Bible. He includes these names among his list of cults: Jehovah's Witnesses, Christian Science, Mormonism, Spiritism, Father Divine, the Theosophical Society, Zen Buddhism, the Church of the New Jerusalem, the Bahai Faith, the Black Muslims, the Unity School and the Worldwide Church of God of H.W. Armstrong. Other writers include: Seventh-Day Adventism, Unitarianism, Rosicrucianism, Transcendental Meditation, the Unification Church, the Hare Krishna Movement, the Divine Light Mission, The Way International and several others.

Each of these cults displays one primary ambition— to satisfy the cry of a person's spirit with a meaningful faith. The grounds of this goal are sincere enough. The principal difficulty, however, is often not easily received.

Most people hold to the ever-popular notion

that if you are sincere in your faith (regardless of your doctrine), and if you don't hurt anyone, then that is all God will require of any of us. God, it would seem from this point of view, has little regard for truth—just so you are earnest in your religious pursuits. But this horrible distortion of the genuine facts is precisely what Satan wants us to believe.

Satan isn't interested in saving someone from God's wrath. Instead, he seeks out a large multitude of avenues in order to divert our attention from God's plans for our salvation through Christ. The Scriptures are straightforward in this matter. Paul emphatically shouts out, *"The god of this age [Satan] has blinded the minds of unbelievers, so that they cannot see the light of the gospel of the glory of Christ"* (2 Cor. 4:4).

Jesus, too, unhesitantly states, *"I am the way and the truth and the life. No one comes to the Father except through me"* (John 14:6). The apostles charged their critics by saying, *"Salvation is found in no one else, for there is no other name under heaven given to men by which we must be saved"* (Acts 4:12)!

The testimony of the Scriptures is simple enough for everyone to understand, if we will listen to it with open minds. The cults present a pseudo-faith, a perverted faith, a deadening faith, a fatal mixture of truth and error. Cults, to put it simply, are not in God's will, but in Satan's plans.

3. *Occultism:* The term "occult" aptly describes the religious experience it houses. The word means "to hide or to conceal from sight." The occult bodies, then, are movements which supposedly have hidden truths at their disposal, providing that the proper steps are followed to discover them. Among this camp of blind guides are the astrologers, witches, Satanists and spiritists (or spiritualists) in general.

The Scriptures strictly forbid any involvement with occult practices. Listen to these weighty words from Moses.

> *When you enter the land the Lord your God is giving you, do not learn to imitate the detestable ways of the nations there. Let no one be found among you who SACRIFICES HIS SON OR DAUGHTER in the fire, who practices DIVINATION or SORCERY, INTERPRETS OMENS, engages in WITCHCRAFT, or CASTS SPELLS, or who is a MEDIUM or SPIRITIST or who CONSULTS THE DEAD. Anyone who does these things is detestable to the Lord, and because of these detestable practices the Lord your God will drive out those nations before you. You must be blameless before the Lord your God.* (Deut. 18:9-14).

If there is any question as to the precise nature of the major words that are employed in this passage (the ones which have been capitalized), then I will now endeavor to be absolutely clear and specific.

The "sacrificing" of a son or a daughter refers to the nearly unbelievable worship of Molech, an Assyrian sun god (see Lev. 18:21; Deut. 12:31). In an act of satanic worship a parent would surrender his baby to a premature death by cremation.

The art of "divination" has reference to all fortunetelling practices. Today this would include such items as these: palm reading, card or tea readings, crystal balls, horoscopes, and Ouija boards.

A "sorcerer" is someone who exercises occult (or mystical) powers. This may include telepathy, clairvoyance and voodoo, to name but a few.

Someone who "interprets omens" is a person who can interpret certain phenomena with a personal flavor. The field of card and tea readings, palm reading, handwriting analysis, and other divination arts fit this classification.

"Witchcraft" may entail casting spells (similar to voodoo), telling the lot of others, and fixing special drinks. It has been estimated there are over 10,000,000 witches in America today! In England it has been estimated that about 80 percent of her young people have had direct contact with this abomination.

"Casting spells" refers to the practice of pronouncing a good sentence (called white magic) or evil sentence (called black magic) upon someone or a group. According to the Scriptures all actions of this sort are satanically inspired (in other words, "white" magic is really "black" magic in disguise). Several years ago a national magazine reported that Los Angeles County in California officially solicited a "good" witch to cast "good" spells upon the county's people. Her first spell was cast before a large audience for a greater sexual vitality in the community!

A "medium" is someone through whom a spirit (or demon) operates. A "spiritist" is a person who has contact with the evil spirits of the world. One of the unique arts of these persons is their supposed ability to "consult the dead." Such visions, trances and seances are strictly satanic shows that are offered to lead a person farther away from the purity of God's perfect Word.

If all of these statements sound as though they are too severe or a little too naive, then consider the Lord's assessment of the so-called harmless practice of astrology.

Let your astrologers come forward, those stargazers who make predictions month by month, let them save you from what is coming. . . . Surely they are like stubble; the

133

*fire will burn them up. They cannot even
save themselves from the power of the flame.*
(Isa. 47:13-14; see also Lev. 20:6, 27)

Enough has been said. If you wish to explore
this matter thoroughly, consult with your local
Christian bookstore. Many excellent volumes
have been recently written on this subject.
Demons in the World Today, by Merrill F. Unger,
is one of the finest books available.

4. *Agnosticism:* This is a term that is frequently misused. The word "agnostic" actually means
"unknowable." Therefore, when someone says he
is an "agnostic," he is stating that the truth about
God cannot be known. At best, according to the
agnostic, we live in a world of mixed religious
opinions with no one able to ultimately discern
what is really a fact from what is really a lie.

The Scriptures, however, will give no comfort
to the agnostic. The Bible states that each person
on this earth knows the true God. This knowledge is revealed through his own personal
creation (Eccles. 3:11), and through the creation
of the world surrounding him (Rom. 1:18-20).

The reason so many persons refuse to acknowledge this fact is because they choose to *"suppress
the truth by their wickedness"* (Rom. 1:18). Jesus
clearly says that his Father will reveal the truth
to anyone who chooses to do God's will (John

7:17). The reason why most people don't know the truth about God is simply due to their apathetic desire to do God's will. The matter is a simple one—God does not disclose himself to those persons who are not sincerely interested in obeying Him.

Again, Jesus said, *"This the verdict: Light has come into the world, but men loved darkness instead of light because their deeds were evil. Everyone who does evil hates the light, and will not come into the light for fear that his deeds will be exposed"* (John 3:19-20).

There are, in actuality, no agnostics in the world. This is merely an escape device some use to hide from God's penetrating light. People who reject the truth of the Scriptures only do so because of a desire to continue in their self-made life styles. They want no one telling them to repent or to change, including God. So, as a cop out they assert that God is not knowable. This is a lie. God is very knowable; He is more knowable and accessible than your next-door neighbor. If you don't know Him, why not get acquainted?!

5. *Atheism:* This is the next step down from agnosticism. Atheism boldly claims that the reason God is unknowable is due to the supposition that He doesn't exist. Much of our modern, evolutionary based sciences operate

135

from this premise. As a result, most school textbooks offer a godless message about the creation, preservation and destiny of this universe. Praise the Lord for Christian schools, especially on the lower levels where a child's values and convictions are first molded!

The atheist has no platform on which to stand. His excuse is like the agnostic's self-erected logic. In the final line the ultimate cause for atheism is a love for darkness, an unteachable spirit in following the truth of the Bible, and an independent attitude.

The Bible calls atheists "fools" (Ps. 14:1). They have no excuse. God is ready and willing to speak to such persons, if they will only listen with a sincere heart.

6. *World Religions:* There are so many different religions in the world that it would be silly to attempt making any list of them and their chief doctrines. It is sufficient to use just one of these religions to illustrate their essential nature, namely Judaism.

The Jewish faith, as wonderful as it is, still must be classified as a dead religion. That is, unless the Jews surrender their hearts to Jesus Christ they must be considered spiritually lost along with the members of other world religions. This crucial fact is pinpointed for us by Paul, a Christian Jew.

*Brothers, my heart's desire and prayer to God
for the Israelites is that they may be saved.
For I can testify about them that they are
zealous for God, but their zeal is not based on
knowledge. Since they did not know the
righteousness that comes from God and
sought to establish their own, they did not
submit to God's righteousness. Christ is the
end of the law so that there may be
righteousness for everyone who believes.*
(Rom. 10:1-4)

The Jews, like many members of other religious bodies, have a "zeal for God." The problem is not sincerity, but "knowledge." Someone may sincerely heat his car for himself and his family by allowing it to warm up in a closed garage. The results of this sincerity, however, can be tragic.

God is not honoring our motives; instead, He is honoring His own Word! We cannot escape this statement. Our hearts may be pure enough, but if our actions do not correspond with God's laws, then there can only be disastrous consequences. Don't evaluate yourself by your sincerity. Examine yourself in the light of God's written Word!

The different religious bodies of the world each share a demonic base, according to the Scriptures (1 Cor. 10:14-22). There is only *one way* to be saved—that is God's way (see John 3:16; 14:6; Acts 4:12). We must come to Jesus, receive

His deep love for ourselves and turn from our sins. We will never be good enough or smart enough to save ourselves. It is useless to even try. That's why Jesus died. He took our failures and sins to the cross with Him, and He paid the price for their offense so that we could exchange our filth for His righteousness. Our salvation is in Christ, only in Christ.

Physical Harm

In addition to the spiritual dimension, Satan is quite busy in messing up people's bodies with mental disorders, moral impurities and physical ailments (see Matt. 12:43-45; Mark 5:1-5; Acts 10:38; etc.).

15

The Work of Satan
with Cities and Nations

The work of Satan surpasses mere individual
involvements. He is also actively engaged in
politics. National concerns play a prominent role
in his many interests.

"The god of this age" (Satan—2 Cor. 4:4) is
incurably ambitious. His schemes invade both
the hearts of people and of nations.

Satan's Past Role in Governments

The classic passage which reveals the depth of
Satan's grasp upon the governments of this world
can be found in Matthew 4:8. Here we read how
Satan tempted Jesus. This is the second temptation.

The devil took him [Jesus] to a very high mountain and showed him all the kingdoms of the world and their splendor. "All this will I give you," he said, "if you bow down and worship me."

Jesus resisted the offer, but He never challenged its validity. Satan *does* exert a powerfully influential role in the control of many national movements. It is not difficult to imagine that Satan possessed such a profound inroad into the political affairs of both Israel and Rome that he personally saw to it that Jesus was killed by the combined labors of these governments (Luke 22:1-2; John 19:1-22; etc.).

From the Old Testament we read of angels who are national princes. That is, they are high-ranking evil angels who operate in Satan's administration with the chief function of influencing national policies. Daniel refers specifically to the angelic prince of Persia and Greece (Dan. 10:13, 20).

Whenever Israel won any military conquest, it was always considered to be due to God's angelic involvement (see chapter 7 for details). But how do the angels influence the outcome of a battle or a war?

We must walk cautiously in this matter. There are only small hints given here and there in the Scriptures, but this much is safe to share. Satan's forces can (1) inhabit the enemies' bodies, giving to them special strength and courage (Mark 5:1-20), and (2) persuade foes of which decisions they ought to make (Rev. 16:12-14; 20:1-3, 7-8).

God's angels, on the other hand, can prevent Satan's hosts from performing these duties. And at the same time they can instruct the nation of His concern about the proper military decisions they need to make. This is precisely what occurred in 2 Kings 6:8-23.

There can be no discounting of these inescapable facts. Our world is run to a larger degree by angels—both good and evil—than we can imagine.

Satan's Present Role in Governments

Israel had (and probably *has*) Michael as her chief guardian angel (Dan. 10:21). Greece and Persia had evil angels exercising oversight in their national politics (Dan. 10:13, 20). This small picture is but one piece in a worldwide puzzle. Above each nation are a few of the highest ranking angels. Above some nations are God's angels; above others are Satan's angels.

The nations of the world, from a spiritual perspective, can be divided into two classes: (1) those guarded and directed by evil angels, and (2) those guarded and directed by God's angels.

It is impossible to say how many nations fall under God's personal protection, and how many may be said to reside under Satan's tight fist. But it does appear realistic to confidently assert that in those countries where the government has taken a strong position against the Christian faith, Satan is actually in control. We need to pray for the Christians in these countries, that their light might be sustained and even enlarged to the degree that these satanic angels might be overthrown and God's angels set up in their place!

A casual look at America's history traces a progressively dim picture. Our land was firmly established on the principles of the Christian faith. As a whole our nation was "one nation under God." But in recent decades a liberalizing and paralyzing effect is becoming evermore evident. We are *not* the nation we used to be. Our values have altered radically. Our general stand on the ground of scriptural authority has all but disappeared in the private sector. We are not a nation under God. Instead, self-will, humanistic philosophy and lukewarm religious traditions are extremely commonplace. We are in sad shape, spiritually.

Unless America turns away from her gross departure from the written Word of God, unless Americans stop their treadmill of self-centeredness and liberalistic education, then America is doomed to experience God's chastening. It happened to Israel when she sinned, and it will happen here, too, unless we repent!

Satan's Future Work in Governments

The subject introduced here is a most complex one. The field of prophecy is filled with satanic activity, especially just prior to Christ's return, and a millennium later, at the close of Jesus' one thousand-year reign upon the earth (see Rev. 6-20).

For the purposes of this small volume it is sufficient to state that in the latter days before the second coming, Satan will attempt to bring the entire world under his leadership. The result will be economic and political chaos. At the Battle of Armageddon it will all be ended, at least temporarily. One thousand years later, for a short time, this lust for power will again be unleashed. After this brief episode, Satan will be forever cast into the lake of fire (Rev. 20:1-10). Look at the chart in chapter 10 for a chronological outline of these events.

16

How You Can Defeat Satan

Satan is not undefeatable. His powers are not limitless. Indeed, the least seasoned Christian has the power to defeat him!

Objective Weapons

In order to defeat the devil we need to be equipped with two types of weapons. The first kind is objective. That is, a weapon given to us by God. It comes to us from the outside. The second style of offense we can use to conquer Satan is subjective. That is, a weapon that emerges from within ourselves.

Both types of weapons—the objective and the subjective—are indispensable for whipping the devil. At the outset, let's consider the objective ammunition God has given to each Christian. Then we will examine our subjective artillery.

1. *The Infallible Word of Truth:* The first thing we receive from God in order to wage a successful combat with Satan is the Word of God. There is no mightier weapon at our disposal than the Scriptures.

In three successive satanic attacks against Jesus, he counterattacked by proclaiming the Word of God (Matt. 4:4, 7, 10). Satan could not stand up against these three spiritual bombs. He was compelled to depart.

Paul calls the Bible *"the sword of the Spirit"* (Eph. 6:17). With this double-edged weapon you can cut your way through a jungle of demonic debris and defend yourself against any assault. This ought to be the greatest possible incentive for pastors to teach their sheep God's Word in its richest possible depths. And at the same time it ought to be an equal incentive for all Christians to get involved in studying the Scriptures with disciplined regularity.

2. *The Name of Jesus:* Another piece of equipment given to each Christian is the use of the name of Jesus. When the disciples returned from one of their missions, John spoke out and said, *"We saw a man driving out demons in your name"* (Luke 9:49).

The disciples were perplexed. They thought that only they had the power required to defeat

Satan. But they had to learn a mighty lesson. Each person who truly follows Christ is furnished with the authority required to overthrow Satan's powers. That authority rests in the use of Jesus' name.

The meaning here is not hard to grasp, though some have missed it. In the book of Acts we read of some people who thought that the use of Jesus' name was simply a magical formula that cast some compelling spell upon a demon. Their attempts in handling demons in this fashion, however, proved to be most embarrassing and fruitless (Acts 19:13-16).

In the same manner some persons suppose that praying in Jesus' name means that you have to conclude each prayer by saying, "In Jesus' name, amen." But not a single time is this ritualistic pattern followed in the entire New Testament. All of the prayers of the New Testament end with either a period or a simple "amen" (see Acts 4:23-30; Eph. 1:15-23, 3:14-21; etc.). There was no liturgical-type formula in Jesus' mind when He instructed His disciples to pray in His name (John 14:13-14).

The proper idea behind the use of Jesus' name is twofold. First, you concede that there is nothing in your name that is capable of conquering Satan. Behind your name (or life) are the scars of sin and the feeble potency of a mere human, in contrast to the superior knowledge and skills of the devil. Second, you acknowledge that in the name (or life) of Jesus is every possible perfection and power. Behind this name is all the authority of heaven and earth (Matt. 28:18).

You cannot lose with a name like that. Your prayers are effective because you approach the Father bearing all the qualities represented in the matchless name of Jesus. And your warfare, too, is successful because of the use of Jesus' name. In a very valid sense you can stand before both Satan or God as though you were Jesus, because you have been authorized the use of His name!

If some rich person gives you the use of his name, then all that stands behind that name becomes available for your utilization as well. What belongs to the rich man now also belongs to you. In like manner, the wealth of heaven is wrapped up in a single name—Jesus (Eph. 1:3-4). When you take that name and use it spiritually, you become greater in power than Satan!

3. *The Blood of Jesus:* Earlier we pointed out that the devil accuses us before God when we sin. Our only defense against this assault is to get rid of our individual sins as soon as possible—preferably the first moment after we recognize we have displeased our Father.

We cannot remove sin from our lives. This is a divine work. We can only confess the reality of its presence and desire its removal. God alone can do the rest. And He is willing to do so.

God's provisions for the cleansing of a believer from the consequences brought about by his sins is the atoning blood of Jesus. If we confess (that is, acknowledge) our sins, then God will be faithful to forgive us and to cleanse us thoroughly (1 John 1:7, 9). And He does so by giving us the righteousness of Christ instead of the punishment we deserve. Through Jesus' blood (the high price He paid for this exchange) we can overcome the evil one, Satan (Rev. 12:9-11).

We don't "plead" the blood, whatever that is supposed to mean. We simply repent. The Lord aplies the blood. That is, He cleanses our record in heaven so that Satan's accusations will carry no weight. If we will do our part, God will surely do His too. We needn't worry about the devil "getting us." God has us in His control, and as long as we walk in the light He provides we need never be afraid (1 John 1:7).

Subjective Weapons

Now we must turn our attention to the subjective weapons of our warfare. We have seen God's provisions above. Below we will explore another aspect of our practice in the use of His weapons.

1. *Submit and Resist:* James writes, *"Submit yourselves, then, to God. Resist the devil, and he will flee from you"* (James 4:7). Here are two commands that cannot be ignored or reversed if

we are to defeat the enemy.

When I consciously experienced the worst satanic assault on my life, I found myself powerless. Perplexed, I couldn't understand why there was no release from all of this reechoing harassment. I had commanded Satan's departure, but it was like telling the sun to turn itself off. Nothing happened. Nothing! Then in came the light. My strategy was wrong, and therefore ineffective. I was attempting to resist before I had submitted to God. I knelt and prayed, confessing my sins to the Lord. When this was finished, I commanded the devil to leave in Jesus' name. The results were fantastic and swift. My mind, which felt as though it were trapped in a cage of demons, was now released and filled with great praises.

The lesson I learned here cannot be measured for its full value. God showed me that before I could *stand up* to the devil, I had to first *kneel* in my spirit to Him! Submission always precedes resistance. It's a principle to be remembered.

2. *Give Satan No Room*: Satan is not permitted to attack believers indiscriminately (Job 1-2; Luke 22:31). We are, generally speaking, shielded from his artillery. But this protection can be weakened, or even removed, by careless living.

Paul warns his readers, "*Do not give the devil a foothold*" (Eph. 4:27; see also 2 Cor. 2:5-11). The particular item Paul had in mind was any failure on our part to resolve interpersonal conflicts before the day was over. Failing to iron out disputes the same day in which they arise is one way we can put a welcome mat at our door for satanic problems. What an incentive this ought to be to maintain wholesome relationships both inside and outside of our homes at all times.

There is a principle here that exceeds the limits of this particular illustration. Any unconfessed sin can give Satan an entry. When Cain was upset at life, the Lord came and spoke these profound words: *"Sin is crouching at your door; it desires to have you, but you must master it"* (Gen. 4:7)!

Here is the supreme point. Satan wants us to sin, so he places opportunities at our very doors in order to entice us. We musn't give him a foothold.

Here are some practical suggestions which can help each of us be better combatants in spiritual warfare:

(a) Keep your eyes away from unwholesome pictures, books, magazines, papers, television shows, plays, movies and the like.

(b) Keep your ears away from unwholesome people, radio programing, records and tapes.

(c) Keep your feet away from unwholesome business enterprises, vocational pursuits, entertainment centers and the like.

No one, naturally, can keep all of these

guidelines all of the time. But we can observe most of them most of the time. And we had better do so, if we want to defeat the devil and be productive in spiritual matters.

This is no advocacy of being a sealed-up hermit who knows nothing of the world about him. It is merely advice to direct us away from unnecessary enticements.

3. *Be Collected:* Peter says, *"Cast all your anxiety on him because he cares for you. Be self-controlled and alert. Your enemy the devil prowls around like a roaring lion looking for someone to devour. Resist him, standing firm in the faith, because you know that your brothers throughout the world are undergoing the same kinds of suffering"* (1 Pet. 5:8-9).

There are two points in this Scripture that deserve our utmost attention. The first matter concerns the kind of person Satan can devour. The second item centers upon how we can conquer the devil.

Not everyone is vulnerable to Satan's attacks. In fact, it seems he is primarily looking for those who are easy prey. He knows he will get nowhere with some Christians, so he challenges those whom he thinks will fall the fastest.

This does not imply that anyone will ever become too strong for Satan to bother with. Instead, it merely suggests that the devil knocks off the easiest people before he concentrates on the more difficult ones.

Peter tells us to be on the ball—*be self-controlled and alert*. Those of us who might be lax or lazy will become prime targets of Satan. He will either render us still weaker or useless in spiritual service.

One way you can defeat the devil is by freeing yourself from every worry. Release yourself from these concerns by giving them to the Lord. He can manage your affairs, all of them. And best of all, He actually wants to help you. Let Him do it.

You cannot worry or doubt and resist at the same time. What a powerful peace is ours when we finally commit everything (our family members, our finances, our vocations, our weaknesses, our troubles, our all) to our heavenly Father! When you can stop trying to figure out how to manage each detail of your life and trust God to handle everything, then it is like sprouting wings and soaring freely above the realm of all anxiety. How wonderful and necessary this ingredient is in combating the enemy.

If you don't possess this freedom or peace, make an appointment to see your pastor for a private consultation or an extended series of counseling sessions. This is vital. Don't neglect it.

If you are a pastor and aren't experiencing this release and joy (and many pastors are not), then talk with another pastor who can be both your confidant and helper. Don't be ashamed or backward. March forward, and get the assistance you need.

4. *Put on the Whole Armor of God:* In the longest treatment found in the Bible on how to successfully oppose Satan, Paul itemizes six elements that are essential for our warfare (Eph. 6:10-18). Here is his list, along with a few brief annotations.

(a) Put on the belt of truth (v. 14). One of God's great attributes is truthfulness (Ps. 33:4, 117:2). No wonder lying and deception are high on His list of prohibitions (Ps. 5:6; Prov. 21:7-8). God seeks truth in those who follow Him. This naturally includes being truthful (or full of truth) in each area of life—before God, your family, your friends, your work or school associates, your church and yourself.

(b) Put on the breastplate of righteousness (v. 14). A righteous person is someone who lives right—in thoughts, words and actions.

(c) Put the gospel of peace on your feet (v. 15). There are no less than five kinds of peace you ought to possess: peace with God (Eph. 2:1-18), peace with yourself (Phil. 4:6-10), peace with fellow Christian soldiers (Phil. 2:1-4), peace with non-Christians (Rom. 12:18), and peace with your circumstances (Phil. 4:11-13; 1 Tim. 6:6-8).

(d) Take up the shield of faith (v. 16). For faith to work you must put it to work. You can't sit on

your faith (shield) and expect it to automatically protect you. It won't. You must take it up. Notice, too, sincerity and faith are *not* synonyms. Sincerity is a matter of attitude; faith is a matter of action. The shield of faith must be actively used to guard your thoughts, speech and actions.

(e) Take the helmet of salvation (v. 17). It is very hard, if not impossible, for a Christian to stride forward until he first has a firm hold on a *know-so salvation.* This includes a salvation from sin's penalty (past), sin's power (present) and sin's presence (future).

(f) Take the sword of the Spirit, the Word of God (v. 17). There are two kinds of armor given to each Christian—one set is defensive (each of those discussed above), and the other is offensive. God's Word is our only offensive weapon. See the first part of this chapter for comments on the Word of God.

It has been stated many times, but it is worth repeating. There is no armor provided for the saint's back. Our combat is face to face, with the confidence that God's weapons are always sufficient to the task. Never turn and run. Confront and conquer.

A Word From Luther

The great reformer Martin Luther believed strongly in a literal devil. A familiar story is told of how Satan appeared to Luther. The monk was so bold as to respond to this appearance by hurling his inkwell at Satan! While this story may or may not be true, it is certain that Luther sensed the power of Satan against him. He also felt the mighty power of Christ at his side. It is from this context that Luther penned one of the most cherished hymns of all time, "A Mighty Fortress Is Our God":

A mighty fortress is our God, A bulwark
    never failing;
Our helper he amid the flood Of mortal ills
    prevailing.
For still our ancient foe Doth seek to work us
woe—His craft and power are great, And,
armed with cruel hate, On earth is not his equal.

Did we in our own strength confide, Our
    striving would be losing,
Were not the right man on our side, The man
    of God's own choosing.
Dost ask who that may be? Christ Jesus, it is
He; Lord Sabaoth, His name, From age to age
the same, And He must win the battle.

And though this world, with devils filled,
    Should threaten to undo us,
We will not fear, for God hath willed His
    truth to triumph through us.
The prince of darkness grim, We tremble not

for him—His rage we can endure, For lo, his
doom is sure: One little word shall fell him.

That word above all earthly powers, No
    thanks to them, abideth,
The Spirit and the gifts are ours Through
    Him who with us sideth.
Let goods and kindred go, This mortal life
also—The body they may kill; God's truth
abideth still: His kingdom is forever! Amen!

PART III:

DEMONS

17

Demonic Reality

Demons are real—as real as the devil himself. And they are evil—as evil as the devil too. While there is only one devil, there are numerous demons. Satan can only be one spot at a time, but his cohorts are everywhere. If you are to take in a complete picture of the invisible realities present in this world, then you must learn about demons.

What Is a Demon?

Aristotle and Plato (famous Greek philosophers of the fourth century before Christ) believed in attendant spirits, which they deemed as being good. Socrates felt his spirit would warn him whenever he was about to make a wrong decision.

The Greek word employed for these spirits is

daimon. It comes from a root word meaning "to know." So, the demons were believed to be intelligent spirits who helped people. The New Testament, however, calls them evil spirits, followers of Satan.

A demon is a spirit (Luke 10:17, 20). That is, they have no flesh or bones (Luke 24:39). Yet they are capable, like the good angels (who are spirits— Heb. 1:14), of assuming a human form (Gen. 6:1-4; Job 1-2; Zech. 3:1).

Demons have the characteristics of a personality. They can speak (Mark 1:24, 34), hear (Mark 5:6-10), feel (Mark 5:7, 12; James 2:19), make decisions (Jude 6), distinguish between the saved and lost people of the earth (Rev. 9:4), and submit to higher authorities (Mark 1:34; 3:22). We should never consider a demon as some blank, impersonal force. They are not things, but persons of a different order from humans. They are a unique "race" of their own.

The Scriptures call these spirits "unclean" (twenty-one times, KJV—Matt. 10:1; etc.), "evil" (twelve times, KJV—1 Sam. 16:14; etc.), and "wicked" (three times, KJV—Matt. 12:45; etc.). There is nothing in their disposition to grant them any measure of praise. They are always opposed to God's will.

With demonic involvement in the affairs of people, it is little wonder that so much immorality is present everywhere. Our eyes and ears are almost constantly bombarded with unwholesome music, television, magazines, books, conversations, and so forth. The influence of demons can be clearly seen in our homes, schools, businesses and government.

The power of the demonic hosts, like the strength of the angelic company, is different from and greater than human capabilities. Their superiority in the mental, physical and magical arenas demands our respect (but not our reverence—Exod. 7:11-12, 8:7; Job 1-2; Mark 5:4; 2 Thess. 2:9; Rev. 13:13; etc.). But we mustn't lose sight of the other side of this truth. Through Christ each believer is made more powerful, in authority, than Satan and all of his host (James 4:7; Rom. 8:37-39; 2 Cor. 10:4).

Are Demons and Fallen Angels the Same?

There is divided opinion among the scholars as to whether or not fallen angels and demons ought to be associated together as referring to the same beings. Some people think they are two totally different types of creatures altogether. Others, however, see them as being identical. (I personally have no strong convictions in either direction.)

The basic reasoning behind envisioning two separate sets of beings is fivefold:

1. Angels have bodies, but demons seek to enter bodies (Mark 5:12; Rev. 16:13-16). While this is undeniable, it must also be confessed that angels,

who are spirits, can enter bodies—just as Satan entered Judas (John 6:70; 13:26-27).

2. Angels fly, but demons walk (Matt. 12:43 KJV). This distinction is more of an inference than an established fact. This Scripture, standing alone, is insufficient evidence to support such a distinction.

3. Angels inhabit the sky, but demons dwell on the earth (Matt. 12:43; Eph. 6:12). Again, this is not clearly established beyond a reasonable doubt. The Scriptures are not explicit in these passages. And when the Bible is bordering on silence, we should do the same.

4. Angels and spirits are presented as being separate entities, according to the Pharisees (Acts 23:8). It does appear that the Pharisees, in some unknown manner, distinguished between angels and spirits. But we do not have God's endorsement of this popular view. We just don't know what the Pharisees believed, and certainly their convictions cannot be accepted without other clear evidence from the Scriptures.

5. There is a huge time gap between Genesis 1:1 and 1:2. The "original" earth was presumably destroyed and later remade (see Job 9:5-7, 38:4-41; Jer. 4:23-26; Isa. 45:18; 2 Pet. 3:4-7). One view holds that the occupants of this first earth were destroyed, but not annihilated—their spirits seemingly still walk the earth as demons. These people, who are said to have lived before the

creation of Adam, are seen as the ancient race of beings (often called cavemen or prehistoric men) who scientists write about today as being the missing link in the evolutionary ladder from ape to men. But these views face the same kind of problems the above points face, namely the absence of direct and explicit evidence from the Bible.

Perhaps the data from the Scriptures is sufficiently clear to establish a distinction between fallen angels and demonic beings, but many are doubtful that this is the case. Regardless of the correct answer, there is, without any doubt, an invisible company of evil spirit-beings who oppose God and who seek to serve Him. Their precise identity (while academically enriching) is insignificant when actually combating them. Our real objective is not to know them better, but to defeat them!

Their Rank

When God, through Jesus, made the angels, He created creatures of varying ranks. That is, their degrees of authority differ. Some were made high officials; others were created with lesser status.

When Satan fell, he took with him at least one-third of all the angelic host (Rev. 12:4). Among these rebels, apparently, were angels of each rank or position in God's kingdom. Here is a listing of the terms that are used in the Scriptures to designate the varying authority levels among the angels.

1. Cherubim (Ezek. 28:14)
2. Seraphim (Isa. 6:1-4)
3. Archangels (Jude 9)
4. Chief princes (Dan. 10:13)
5. Princes (Dan. 10:13, 20)
6. Thrones (Col. 1:16)
7. Authorities (Col. 1:16; 2:10)
8. Powers (Eph. 1:21; 6:12)
9. Dominions (1 Cor. 15:24)
10. Rulers (Eph. 6:12)
11. Watchers (Dan. 4:13-23 KJV)

It is impossible to be certain of the exact order of rank which exists in these designations. It may well be, too, that certain of these titles are equivalent to different titles used by other biblical writers.

This information does tell us that the demonic hosts operate according to a chain-of-command arrangement, with lesser authorities being in subjection to higher-ranking members. Every successful operation in life is managed according to a chain of command.

Their Number

It has already been stated that one-third of the heavenly creatures fell along with Satan. The Scriptures give us no hint as to just how many this entails.

In the fourteenth century the number of angels was said to be 301,655,722. Others, however, have set this number at 6,666 legions of angels with 6,666 angels in each legion—that would make 44,435,556 angels. Some writers have stated that you can't count them because they multiply like flies! According to the Talmud (an ancient Jewish commentary) there are 7,405,926 demons. It is not stated how this figure was obtained. The Cardinal Bishop of Tusculum, in the fifteenth century, estimated the demon count at 133,306,668. From a collection of various writings some 103 fallen angels have been named.

With all of this speculation available, one point is certain—we don't have any idea how many demons Satan commands. We can only safely say that God's angels, when seen by several saints, were considered countless (Dan. 7:10; Rev. 5:11). Therefore, one-third of this count (the number that fell—Rev. 12:4) would make for a large demonic army. On the positive side, however, let's never forget that for each angelic follower of Satan there are two such creatures following the will of God! That's important to keep in perspective.

Their Locations

The fallen angels are not all dwelling in one central site. Neither can it be said that they are all in one general area. Actually, fallen angels can be found in four different locations.

1. Some fallen angels are bound in Tartarus (a chamber in the lowest regions of hades—2 Pet. 2:4). These angels were placed there apparently after their cohabitation with women on the earth (see Gen. 6:1-4; Jude 6). These angels will remain in this prison until the time for their resurrection and judgment. This will occur at the close of the millennial reign of Christ (Rev. 20:7-10).

2. Four fallen angels are said to be bound in the Euphrates River (Rev. 9:13-21). The cause for this situation is not stated. They will in the future be released to oversee an army that will kill one-third of the human race. This devastating march of death will transpire immediately prior to the second coming of Jesus Christ.

3. In the abyss at this present hour is a numberless host of demonic creatures awaiting their release (Rev. 9:1-11). Again, the timing for their departure is just prior to the return of Jesus. In the very last days there will be multiplied misery for earth's residents—especially for the non-Christians—for Satan's army will be granted countless fresh recruits. The gates of hell will be opened wide in the final days before Christ's return.

4. Finally, the rest of the fallen angels may be found in the sky (opposing God's angels) and on the earth (opposing God's people). See Ephesians 6:10-12 and the following chapter of this book for further details.

18

Demonization and Exorcism

One of the chief occupations of the demonic world is to harrass people. Often this entanglement is brief and without serious consequences. At other periods, however, demonic involvement is sharply intense and exceedingly consequential. In this chapter we want to expose the works of demons and how they can be successfully overcome.

Demonization or Demon-possession?

Each of the nine translations of the Scriptures with which I am familiar always renders the Greek word *daimonizomai* with these two words: "demon possession." The exact cause for this translation is not clear. Perhaps the consistent usage of the rendering since Tyndale's translation in the 1500's has caused it to be rooted so deeply in our minds that another translation seems unnecessary. Still, this notion may not convey the fuller picture, as we shall see.

The primary difficulty resides in the meaning of "possession." If a demon is in "possession" of a body, then presumably God cannot "possess" it too. There can only be one owner (or possessor) at any given time. In other words, this translation leads us to conclude (and many have done just this) that a Christian cannot be demon "possessed" because he is "possessed" by God. Theoretically, the Holy Spirit and evil spirits cannot co-possess anyone. This argument may sound logical, but, in fact, it is without any scriptural warrant.

Virtually all scholars who have written on the subject of demons in recent years have caught this subtle error and pointed it out in their writings. The Greek term should be translated "demonized." The idea suggested in this word is far more precise. It simply denotes demonic influence or control, without any thought of ownership (or possession).

This translation also serves to clear up another problem. For a long period it has been taught that some people are oppressed by demons, others are obsessed by them, and still others are possessed by these evil spirits. Again, the pure language of the Bible is against this tri-level gradation of demonization. According to the Scriptures a person is either demonized or he is not demonized. There is no thought of the degree of demonization within the term; such a conveyance is unnecessary.

Five terms are used to refer to demonic influence in the King James Version of the Bible:

1. You can be *vexed* by demons (Matt. 15:22; Luke 6:18; Acts 5:16).

2. You can be *oppressed* by demons (Acts 10:38).

3. You can be *with* (Greek: *en*) a demon; that is, you can be in the scope of their influence or control (Mark 1:23, 5:2).

4. You can *have* a demon indwelling your body (Matt. 11:18; Mark 7:25, 9:17; Luke 4:33, 8:27, 13:11; John 7:20, 8:48-49, 52, 10:20-21).

5. You can be *demon possessed/demonized*; that is, under demonic influence or control, to varying degrees (Matt. 4:24, 8:16, 28, 33, 9:32; 12:22, 15:22; Mark 1:32, 5:15, 16, 18; Luke 8:36).

These five usages are synonymous. To *have* a demon is the same as being *vexed* by a demon. And so forth.

A careful examination of these passages will disclose to you the fact that no distinction is made between internal activities (supposedly, possession) and external activities (supposedly, oppression). In each instance the demonic work occurs *within* the person under attack.

171

Neither are differing degrees of influence suggested by the use of any of these terms. And finally, there is no attempt to distinguish between Christian and non-Christian demonization. Everyone is a possible subject for these assaults.

Can Christians Be Demonized?

From the above point it should be clear that both Christians and non-Christians can be influenced by demons. It should also be plain to see that demons do not work *in* lost people and merely *on* saved persons. Their approach is the same with each party— they come *in* to do their work, whatever it is.

On the following page is a chart to assist you in discovering the reality of demons and methods they employ. Carefully read each item. Pray over them.

Demonization or Flesh?— Discernment is Needed

After examining the chart, which focuses on the fifteen areas of demonic influence, you may feel that virtually everything you do that is wrong is caused by demons. But this impression is false. If there is anything as disturbing as an ignorance of demonization, it is our seeing these evil spirits in everything, including the kitchen sink. Either extreme is dangerous; balance is necessary.

FIFTEEN FOCAL POINTS IN DEMONIC ATTACKS

THE AREA	THE REFERENCES
1. Sickness	1. Luke 13:10-16
2. Speech	2. Matt. 16:21-23
3. Departure from faith	3. Luke 22:31-34; 1 Tim. 5:9-15; 2 Tim. 2:24-26
4. Hypocrisy	4. Acts 4:32-5:11
5. Sexual relationships	5. 1 Cor. 7:3-5
6. Idolatry	6. 1 Cor. 10:16-22
7. Unforgiveness	7. 2 Cor. 2:6-11
8. Thoughts	8. 2 Cor. 10:3-5; 11:3
9. Cults and/or Liberal "Christianity"	9. 2 Cor. 11:13-15
10. Witchcraft and/or the Occult	10. Deut. 18:9-14; 1 Cor. 10:20
11. Lies and Anger	11. Eph. 4:25-27
12. Premature ambition	12. 1 Tim. 3:6-7
13. Deception	13. 1 Tim. 4:1
14. Persecution	14. Rev. 2:9-10
15. All kinds of sin: evil desires, idolatry, pleasure seeking, immorality, testing God, grumbling and pride.	15. 1 Cor. 10:1-12; 1 Pet. 5:8

We don't need a demon's influence in order to sin. I don't know if that fact is comforting or not. Nevertheless, it is true. We can sin by ourselves, without any help. By our very own natures we tend to be rascals. Paul itemizes, in three separate listings, some forty-five works of the flesh.

Galatians 5:19-21

1. adultery
2. fornication
3. uncleanness
4. lasciviousness (lust)
5. idolatry
6. sorcery (witchraft)
7. hatred
8. strife
9. jealousy (emulations)
10. wrath
11. factions (dissension)
12. seditions (insubordination)
13. heresies (selfish ambitions)
14. envyings (covetousness)
15. murders
16. drunkenness
17. reveling (wild partying)

Colossians 3:5-9

18. evil desires
19. anger
20. malice (spite)
21. blasphemy
22. filthy communication
23. lying

24. lesbianism
25. homosexuality
26. loss of God's thoughts
27. all unrighteous-ness
28. maliciousness
29. deceit
30. malignity (evil disposition)
31. whisperers (slanderers)
32. backbiters
33. haters of God
34. insolent (violent)
35. proud
36. boasters
37. inventors of evil
38. disobedient to parents
39. without under-standing
40. promise breakers
41. without natural affections
42. implacable
43. unmerciful
44. wickedness
45. take pleasure in sin

This listing should make it abundantly plain that if Satan and demons never existed, there would still be a vital need for Calvary. No one has ever made us sin, not even once. We sin by choice, by habit and by ignorance. Each of us do this, and more regularly than most of us might suppose.

But now arises a thorny question: If the demons can influence me to sin, and if I can also sin without their encouragement, how can I tell when the inclination toward sin is fleshly or demonic? In other words, how can I discern between demons attacking me and my flesh generating its own disobedience?

The answer which best satisfies this dilemma is simple. If our problem is fleshly based, then it will yield to repentance, prayer for strength and self-discipline (see 1 Cor. 9:24-27; Phil. 4:11-13; 2 Tim. 1:7; 1 Pet. 4:1-11; etc.). This does not mean all of our fleshly problems can be whisked away in a sparkling moment; but it does mean that the root of our sinfulness can be dealt with competently and confidently.

On the other hand, if our problem is demonically based, then we must submit ourselves (along with our problem) to God and resist the devil with a strong, positive, verbal assault. Boldly renounce his tyranny, and proclaim Christ as Commander in charge of your life. Stand on the promises of victory (see John 10:10; James 4:7; 1 Pet. 5:7-8).

Quite frankly, we don't always know which area— the flesh or demons—is giving us trouble. So, to be on the safe side of things, I have found it successful to enact both defenses—subduing both enemies in a full sweep. My problem may not have been demonic, but I didn't waste any energy to be certain.

One other tip you may find profitable is this one: when you have sincerely committed a matter to the Lord (no matter how large or small), adamantly refuse to accept any thoughts but praise regarding the issue. If God has your difficulty (and He does if you've asked Him in faith to take it—1 Pet. 5:7), then you couldn't find a better solution if you had one billion dollars and one thousand years to find one. God, the all-loving, all-powerful, all-wise, and all-sovereign Lord of heaven and earth, will assuredly do what is best with your difficulty. Praise the Lord!

Exorcism

People often shun this very practical element in the teaching on demons. This is regrettable because it is here that you can be greatly helped—not to mention be greatly used in helping others.

At the outset, let me state that there is no encouragement here for anyone to become a self-appointed exorcist! Some people have really gotten out of line through an excessive emphasis upon the deliverance ministry. Again, balance is the key. We must neither overstress nor understress the role of exorcism in the believer's walk with Christ.

When a believer sincerely struggles with a particular sin, it is not unnatural to assume he may need deliverance from one or several attacking demons. One fine Christian man I know had an almost irresistible drive to read the literature of a cult. After prayerfully confronting this problem, the man became convinced that the source of his difficulty was demonic. So we prayed with him, and then commanded the demons to depart. The gentleman gave three deep sighs and confidently said, "I am free!" He never returned to the books. The desire was gone because the source for the desire was uprooted.

One evening in a Bible study, a Christian lady related how she was compulsively driven to surrender her body for sexual gratification. We prayed for her, harmonizing with her desire to be rid of this lust. At some point I commanded the demons behind this intense drive to come out of her. She instantly collapsed and began to weep. In a moment she looked up with a bright smile and said, "It's gone! It's gone!" She was delivered.

Generally, the privilege of exorcism is not spooky at all. When our warfare with Satan's hosts is properly understood, this ministry is a needed and desirable part of one's Christian service to another.

We need to pray for each other. We may also need to command Satan to depart from someone we love. This, too, is a Christian ministry. See the chart on the following pages.

Why Jesus Came to Earth

Have you considered the fact that Jesus came to this planet to do more than provide a bridge from earth to heaven? He did. Jesus marched His way through life with another ambition. He came to defeat the devil.

Since the initial fall of Satan it has been in God's plans to someday crush him beneath Jesus' feet (Gen. 3:15). That day has arrived. Jesus has stripped Satan of his power. We can walk triumphantly in the footsteps laid before us by Jesus. We do not fight for victory, but from our position of victory.

> Since the children have flesh and blood, he [Jesus] too shared in their humanity so that by his death he might destroy him who holds the power of death—that is, the devil— and free those who all their lives were held in slavery by their fear of death. (Heb. 2:14-15)

> God made you alive with Christ. He forgave us all our sins, having canceled the written code, with its regulations, that was against us and that stood opposed to us; he took it away, nailing it to the cross. And having disarmed the powers and authorities, he made a public spectacle of them, triumphing over them by the cross. (Col. 2:13-15)

> The reason the Son of God appeared was to destroy the devil's work. (1 John 3:8)

EXORCISM IN THE BIBLE

Scripture	Victim(s)	Key Phrase	Believer or Unbeliever	Symptom(s)
Matt. 4:24	All	Possessed	?	Sickness
Matt. 12:22	Man	Possessed	?	Blindness and muteness
Matt. 15:22-28	Daughter	Cruelly Possessed	?	Vexation
Mark 7:25		Had		
Mark 1:23-26	Man	With	?	Uncleanness
Luke 4:33-35		Had		Impurity
Luke 4:40-41	All	Possessed	?	Sickness
Matt. 8:16				
Luke 6:17-18	Multitude	With	?	Vexation
Luke 8:26-39	Man	Had	?	Extraordinary strength, wild, screaming self-torture, naked-ness, mental disorder
Matt. 8:28-34		Possessed		
Mark 5:2-20		With		

180

EXORCISM IN THE BIBLE (2)

Scripture	Victims	Key Phrase	Believer or Unbeliever	Symptom(s)
Luke 9:38-42 Mark 9:14-29 Matt. 17:14-18	Son	Had	?	Fear, screaming pain, foaming at mouth, un-controlled body movement, mute-ness, grinding teeth, suicidal impulses
Luke 11:14	Man	?	?	Muteness
Luke 13:10-16	Woman	Had/Bound With	Believer	Crippled body
Acts 5:14-16	All		?	Sickness/Vexation
Acts 8:5-7	Many	Had	?	Sickness
Acts 16:16-18	Woman	Had	?	Fortunetelling
Acts 19:11-12	?	?	?	Sickness

PART IV

BOOK REVIEW

19

Angels on Assignment

Are angels appearing today, bringing messages from God? Is Gabriel on assignment to instruct certain people in the Body of Christ concerning God's unfolding plan for the world? Are these unprecedented experiences to be shared with the Church-at-large, as though they were a broader and necessary revelation from God?

Roland H. Buck thinks so. He states that he has had eighteen visitations from Gabriel (along with other angels, including the familiar Michael and the unknown Chrioni). Mr. Buck says, "The most outstanding and thrilling thing that has ever taken place in my life has been the angelic visitations which have occurred during the last two years" (starting on June 18, 1978). The result of these encounters has been (among other things) the publication of a book entitled, *Angels on Assignment* (Hunter Books, Houston, Texas, 1979).

Sales for the book thus far seem to indicate a wide interest in angelic phenomena. The reception of his writing has been quite strong. But it has also aroused considerable concern from numerous Christians. There are some serious questions raised by this book and these need biblical answers. And for many sincere Christians, the background to adequately evaluate the validity of Mr. Buck's episodes with the angels is limited.

This chapter is an analysis of Mr. Buck's encounters, along with an evaluation of his interpretation of these experiences. The objective here is to deal with the facts as they are presented, and not to degrade, in any manner, the figure behind them—namely, Roland H. Buck.

Mr. Buck is a pastor in the Assemblies of God. For the past twenty years he has served Central Assembly of God Christian Life Center in Boise, Idaho, where the average Sunday morning attendance is well over one thousand people. According to Homer B. Walkup, District Superintendent of the Assemblies of God of southern Idaho, Pastor Buck has a sincere ministry of proven faithfulness and fruitfulness. We have no reason to doubt these statements. Again, let me emphasize

186

that the stress here is to have a confrontation with the principles involved, and not with an individual.

The Matter of Authority

Life is run by authority. If there were no authority then all of life would be a horrible chaotic mess. If there were no authority then each person would believe and practice what was right in his own eyes. Should someone happen to believe it was all right to kill babies, then where there was no authority to declare this an unauthorized action, it would be considered "legal."

You can see how dreadful a state is created if any one person assumes absolute authority. This is why we, collectively, pass legislation to assure the security and well-being of the whole of society. Then we establish what we call "authorities" to administer these regulations. To the degree that these authorities achieve success, we have peace in our world.

Authority appears in various levels. First, there is the three-pronged authority structure in the home: (1) husbands are to submit to Christ; (2) wives are to submit to husbands; and (3) children are to submit to parents (1 Cor. 11:3; Eph. 6:1).

Next, there is authority in our society. Each of us is to obey the laws of our land (Rom. 13:1-7). Additionally, the principle of authority can be found in the employee/employer relationship; the Church/Christ relationship; the sheep/shepherd relationship, and so forth. Every area of life is fixed on the principles of authority.

When it comes to the Christian, the issue of authority is critical. The Scriptures exhort us to submit to authority structures found at home, school, on the job, in the church and in society at large. But ultimately we are forced to draw a line between what is the proper use of authority and its abuse.

Christians have an authoritative rule book—the Bible. We are not authorized to break its codes, even if it means breaking a lesser authority in our society. The Scriptures are the Supreme Court for the Christian. There is no higher court of appeal. What the Bible says stands.

Now comes the application, with reference to the book, *Angels on Assignment*. Can any statement found in this book hold a superior authority to the Scriptures? Emphatically—"NO!" Regardless of how persuasive any experience may be, it can never, in any degree, supercede the authority of the Holy Bible.

Fortunately, Mr. Buck does not assert that his book is intended to usurp the message of the Scriptures. Indeed, he is quite emphatic that nothing he has experienced or taught has the slightest threat of jeopardizing the superior role of the Bible.

The Matter of Extrabiblical Data

While Pastor Buck contends that nothing he says challenges the authority of the Scriptures, his extrabiblical statements (that is, his teachings for which there is no direct scriptural evidence) have the effect of possessing an authority equal to the Scriptures themselves. In other words, it is difficult to harmonize statements like these:

1. *"I have not added to, or taken away from the Word of God, but the Spirit [through angelic visitations] has opened my eyes to things I had not previously seen, just as he reveals truths to any believer who searches the Word"* (*Angels on Assignment*, pp. 13-14).

2. *"Through the inspiring messages brought by angels, the Lord has given me some beautiful insights that I could never have learned by intensive study"* (p. 37).

The former statement (#1) is acceptable; but the latter proposition (#2) is unauthorized. The second statement gives us the declaration that the teaching from angels is necessary in order to grasp (at least some of the points of) God's Word. But this is not true. John writes, *". . . his [the Holy Spirit's] anointing teaches you about all things"* (1 John 2:27; see also v. 20).

This does not mean that angels have never said

anything to help someone understand God's words. They *have* (read Daniel, Zechariah and Revelation). The point here is simply that angels do not conduct Bible studies for Christians in order to unravel previously undiscernible Scriptures. Stated slightly differently (for the sake of clarity), angels have never—in the totality of the Scriptures, 2,100 years—come to someone and explained to him or to her the meaning of a certain passage. In the cases of Daniel, Zechariah and John the angels who spoke with them were merely explaining a current revelation God had given to them. This is not only illumination for the prophet, but a canon-type revelation as well (which, naturally, properly fits itself into the sacred Scriptures). This new type of "insight" for today strikes a curious note of doubt in our minds.

With direct regard to the extrabiblical data presented in Mr. Buck's book, here is a list of the matters not supported by direct scriptural evidence.

1. The identity of the angel who stood by Joshua, Zechariah and Paul is stated as being Chrioni (p. 178). Elsewhere this angel is said to be Gabriel (p. 102).

2. The Holy Spirit monitors the whole earth, picking up signals everywhere at once. He also is responsible to send out orders to the angels (pp. 40, 93).

3. There are different types of angels—praise angels, worship angels, ministering angels, and warring angels (p. 41).

4. Gabriel has access to the timetable of everything that has been predicted, except the second coming of Christ (p. 44).

5. The size of the angels (at least the one Mr. Buck saw) were seven feet tall (or more) and weighed close to 400 pounds (p. 45).

6. Chrioni recalls the details of how he and the other angels delivered Israel from Egypt and other enemies (pp. 46-47).

7. It is in the throne room where all the secrets of the universe are kept (p. 51).

8. There are billions of files in heaven's archives (p. 52).

9. God gave to Paul a bigger brain capacity than normal (p. 53).

10. Abraham and Sarah had a real feeling for those less fortunate than they (p. 54).

11. God records no failure in heaven (p. 54).

12. Everything in heaven is on a light, happy and relaxed basis (p. 55).

13. Black holes in space were first announced to Pastor Buck, prior to their discovery by space probes in 1978 (pp. 56-57).

14. There is an area (a type of hallway) between our permanent abiding place in heaven or hell and earth, a place from which we can be brought back (pp. 58-59).

15. The angels are on every hill, every tree, and even in the holes of the ground, looking for men who are trying to hide from God (p. 79).

16. Gabriel's function is to see that God's plans are fulfilled (p. 101).

17. There is a book in heaven which records man's dealing with man (p. 103).

18. Satan is unaware of what is going to happen in the future; neither can he read minds. This makes him extremely nervous (p. 169).

19. Gabriel is the leading angel; therefore, he coordinates all angelic activities as he stands in God's presence (p. 169).

20. Michael is the leader of all the warring angels (p. 170).

21. Chrioni is the captain of the Lord's hosts (p. 170).

22. Jericho's thick walls were pushed "down" into the ground, not tipped over (pp. 178-179).

23. The angels of God are unlimited in power (p. 183).

24. There is as much excitement in heaven today, says Gabriel, as there was when Jesus first came to earth (p. 192).

There are other points that might be raised, but these represent the most obvious matters of question.

Our first impression of these extrabiblical "revelations" might be somewhat passive. That is, we might say something like this: "Who am I to judge another person's experience? Couldn't God speak to us today and say these things? Pastor Buck hasn't denied any of the cardinal doctrines. Besides, none of these additional revelations are really significant; they just help convey what the Bible is saying. Right?" WRONG.

Here is the crux of the issue. Some of Pastor Buck's statement *are* unquestionably in error. Let me point out just several certain mistakes that are supposedly directly from God.

1. The angel who stood by Zechariah is said in one place to be "Gabriel" (p. 102). Elsewhere, this angel is said to be Chrioni (p. 29, 178). This is a clear contradiction. Certainly God does *not* contradict himself. Pastor Buck must be confused.

2. According to the Scriptures the Holy Spirit is nowhere said to be in charge of the angels, as Mr. Buck suggests (p. 40, 93). This position of authority belongs to Jesus Christ (Matt. 28:18; Col. 1:16; 2 Thess. 1:7-10).

3. God *does* record failure in heaven, of saints and of sinners alike (p. 55; 1 Cor. 3:10-15; 2 Cor. 5:10; Rev. 20:11-15).

4. Black holes in space have been a topic of astronomy for over twenty-five years, not just the past two or three (pp. 56-57). The field of astronomy has been a hobby of mine for the past year, and my research has repeatedly made this

point plain.

5. Why would Satan not know the future? The demons once responded to Jesus, "*Have you come here to torture us before the appointed time?*" (Matt. 8:29). Apparently they were aware of their future lot. Additionally, when Satan will be cast to the earth by Michael and his angels, the Scriptures record that he will be filled with fury, "because he knows that his time is short" (Rev. 12:12). This reference sounds like Satan knows at least part of the future. Finally, because the devil can quote Scripture (Matt. 4:1-11), he must be aware of the prophetic words regarding himself. It is highly unlikely to think otherwise.

6. While there are some biblical scholars who do not accept the teaching that Jesus is "the angel of the Lord" or "the captain of the Lord's host," no one would identify him as being Chrioni, except Mr. Buck (p. 170).

7. The pushing down of Jericho's walls (into the ground rather than tipping over onto the ground) has neither the support of the Scriptures nor the backing of archeological discoveries. In fact, the only findings of this old city, which existed during the late Bronze Age (the period of Joshua's conquest), are the foundation of a single wall and one square yard of a house floor. None of the city walls or other structures have survived the erosion of the thirty-five centuries since this event. If the angels did push these walls down,

like an elevator, we have no proof of such a matter.

8. Are God's angels the possessors of limitless power (p. 183)? No. Only God is all-powerful. None of God's creation is equal to the Creator.

If God doesn't lie or deceive—and He does not—then I am forced to state that either Pastor Buck misinterpreted his experiences or he did not truly hear from God. Let's consider these options, along with other considerations below.

The Matter of Private Interpretation

No one is disturbed by a person's diligent study of God's Word. Indeed, such devotion is commanded by the Lord (2 Tim. 2:15). We esteem such persons and give to them honor double to that of all other persons (1 Tim. 5:17).

Still, when any diligent teacher of the Scriptures asserts that his views are absolutely correct because God told him so, then our eyebrows are raised with a serious concern. Having positive convictions are a necessary part of our Christian walk, but regarding these convictions as though they were as inspired as the Scriptures themselves is another matter altogether.

The Scriptures *are* inspired. We accept this categorically and resolutely. There is no wavering from this assertion (2 Tim. 3:16). On the other hand, our interpretation of God's written Word is subject to a lesser status. No one can legitimately say that his views are always without error. People can and do misinterpret God's intended meaning in the Scriptures.

This does not in any degree imply that the Scriptures are unknowable or that we should not listen to teachers explain the sense of Scripture. Instead, all that is being said here is the crucial fact that we recognize there is no one person, or group of persons, who hold errorless interpretations of God's Word! All Christians hold identical convictions on the major elements of the Bible's doctrines (this is necessary to be a Christian), but beyond the few absolute tenets there is ample divergency of interpretations to keep the best students of the Bible humble.

Today, regardless of how spiritual and diligent we become, we will still never see more than the tip of the iceberg. Our vision is limited because our perspective is restricted. Naturally, this is all in God's present plans. We are not all-knowing, and never will be in this life. In fact, at our very best we should be so honored to *see through a glass, darkly*" (1 Cor. 13:12 KJV). This doesn't imply that everything about life is fuzzy. No, it isn't. But it does compel us to recognize that there is a great deal more to each story of life than we presently perceive.

Our minds may be renewed (Rom. 12:2; Col. 3:10). And our understanding may be extremely enriched, even up to the final hour of our deaths. But our knowledge will never be complete or perfect, regardless of how long we live or how many experiences we have.

The Baptists don't hold all the truth. Neither do the Catholics. The Episcopalians are not errorless. There are empty spaces of knowledge among the Methodist, Presbyterian, Nazarene, Lutheran, Disciples of Christ, Assemblies of God, Independent, and Alliance bodies. None of them are flawless. They see, like everyone else, "through a glass, darkly." This fact is true across the board. No one is excluded. What an incentive this ought to be for us to look diligently, and to find what is good in each of our brothers and sisters, and not to trust exclusively in any of the particular labels we might wear.

Now, finally, to my main point—the views in the book, *Angels on Assignment*, are presented, regrettably, with the air of absolute accuracy. Mr. Buck confidently contends that what he says is exactly the mind and heart of God. Here are a few illustrations of this boldness.

"*God made it very clear to me that I am to share what happened in my life, so I am passing on [the] . . . messages I have been given*" (p. 13).

"*He [the angel] discussed the unfolding plan of God for the entire world*" (p. 20).

"*'I [God] want to give you [R.H. Buck] . . . an "overlay" of truth.' In a split second of eternity, we* went from *Genesis to Revelation*" (p. 51).

"*During this visit, God truly gave me a glorious glimpse of the hidden secrets of the universe; of matter, energy, nature and space . . . I could see all the pieces fit together in what God was doing*" (p. 52).

"*He [God] has revisited me over and over again by means of these heavenly angelic beings with messages for today's world*" (p. 70).

"*Early one morning the Holy Spirit said, 'Write, preserve the words I have spoken to you. They shall become light to many'*" (p. 93).

"*I also feel a profound responsibility to bring to the world the truths which God has placed upon my heart*" (p. 133).

"*Gabriel told me to share this news*" (p. 168).

"*God is doing something special now! He has chosen a place to pour out his message, his word and his special insight for this day, just as he did in Daniel's time. There is no question about it, Boise, Idaho, is a touchdown place for angelic beings*" (p. 171).

Certainly no one would squabble over the impact that accompanies any supernatural experience. We are penetrated to the very depths of our being; not a single cell of our bodies is left untouched. We will never be quite the same after these precious experiences. But we must also consider the impact and influence these glorious happenings have on others.

Some of the natural difficulties arising from any spiritual experience are these:

1. Was my experience, despite its excitement, truly from God?
2. How should I interpret this experience?
3. Was this experience only for me, or was it for others too?
4. Should I share any or all of this experience with others?
5. To what degree does my background (theology, vocation, previous experiences, education, family life, etc.) influence or get mixed in with the recording and retelling of this experience?

It is here, in these five areas, that some people have had trouble. In their zeal for God they have unintentionally distorted the purpose or meaning of their experiences. For instance, a Christian is spared an operation for some ailment because of a person's prayer for their healing. Marvelous! This has happened! But what has also sometimes happened after this event is an unintentional misinterpretation that *all* Christians can avoid surgery *if* they will only pray and believe God for their healing. The experience was true enough, but the proper understanding of the event was distorted.

When everything has been said, there are only three possible options available to us in exploring our experiences. They either come from (1) God, (2) Satan, or (3) self. There is no other alternative.

When we look at Mr. Buck's statements in this light, we are hesitant to assert that they come from God because of the extrabiblical and unfounded claims resident in them. God is not adding anything to the Bible today—nothing (Eph. 2:20ff; Jude 3; Rev. 22:18-19; etc.). We are reluctant, also, to boldly state that each of his encounters are demonic, though this, admittedly, is possible. Finally, we are motivated to support the idea, as Mr. Buck himself confesses (p. 58), that his experiences are actually hallucinations.

Added statements, not found in Mr. Buck's book, but discovered by Christian Research Institute (P.O. Box 500, San Juan Capistrano, CA 92693), make the above conclusion even more convincing. Write them for details.

The listener of R.H. Buck's messages may feel compelled to either accept all of or reject all of his statements. But this is unfair. If this rule were strictly enforced on all speakers, then there wouldn't be anyone to whom we could listen and learn. Each of us unknowingly passes along elements of error in our speech. Mr. Buck is no exception. We must, then, hear the parts of what he says that are unquestionably true (which, by the way, happen to be quite a few), receive them warmly, and rejoice in his witness. We must evaluate Pastor Buck's ministry with the same kind of spiritual and loving discernment we would hope to receive from others who might evaluate our own labors.

My duty is to love Pastor Buck always, and to correct him gently (though with a firm authority) when he is found to be in error. This has been my ambition in the preceding pages.

Evaluating Supernatural Experiences

The Scriptures exhort us to examine all things (1 Cor. 2:15; 1 Thess. 5:21). We mustn't naively accept everything bearing God's name. There *is* a spirit of error and deception that would endeavor to seduce believers. We, therefore, must constantly stand on guard to refute lies and to proclaim the pure Word of truth.

Yet, the question remains: How do I evaluate a supernatural experience? How can I discern what comes from God and what proceeds from the flesh or Satan?

First, let's consider some of the false (or untrustworthy) standards we might use in this evaluation process:

1. *Personality:* Some very warm and sincere people embrace the devil's lies. The personality of a party cannot be used exclusively to determine who is genuine and who is not. Many persons have been swayed by the charisma of a person's life (like the pathetic followers of Jim Jones in the Guyana massacre). We cannot use

personality as a test for truth.

2. *Converts:* Sometimes we are practically taught that the success factor of a work can be measured in its fruit—that is, in its number of converts. We almost instinctively say that so-and-so is doing just fine—look at his membership grow. Statistics, however, aren't true gauges. Two of the most rapidly growing religious bodies in America are cults (Mormons and Jehovah's Witnesses)! Certainly this fast numerical incline cannot be interpreted as a sign of God's blessings. This notion can be carried to extremes, even in local evangelical churches.

3. *Finances:* This point is like the one above. Numerous cults raise multiplied millions of dollars each year, but not because God is behind them. Elsewhere, in local churches, when finances are good, we naturally think God is with us. But the financial barometer is an unsafe guide. Some of God's choice saints have experienced poverty (Mark 12:41-44; Phil. 4:11-12). Indeed, the Lord instructs us to guard ourselves from the money-standard trap (Matt. 6:19-33; 1 Tim. 6:6-8).

4. *The Supernatural:* Jesus warned there would be many who would perform various kinds of miracles in His name, but who are not sent from Him (Matt. 7:21-23). There *are* false spiritual gifts. A person's words cannot always be confirmed by accompanying signs. We must check

still further.

5. *Happiness:* If we think that all Christians are happy, then we aren't getting around. Numerous genuine believers are *not* happy much of the time. We may conclude that they are unhappy because of some lack of personal priorities or discipline, but the fact remains—not all saints are smiling. On the other hand, not all sinners are sad. There *is* pleasure in sin, even if it is temporary (Heb. 11:25). It is possible to be happy and not be spiritual. Some people really get "blessed" at meetings where the truth is not honored. We can't say that because a particular meeting made many people feel good, however, that it was ordained of the Lord.

Now this leads us to some pretty important conclusions. Despite the fact that God very well may grant a body of believers with a pastor of an exceptional personality, and give to it many converts, much money, all of the spiritual gifts, and profound joy, these ingredients, in themselves, are not proofs that He is supporting their labors (since the cults can raise the same evidence in support of their supposedly God-ordained practices).

Ultimately there is only one certain method for ascertaining the validity of any person's speech or experiences—they must concur with the Scriptures! Any person or group that claims to expose the truth but fails to align their statements with the written Word of God (Genesis-Revelation) is deceived.

Many erring persons, to complicate matters, use the Bible as their defense. This is the case with the Mormons, Jehovah's Witnesses, many liberals, and other offbeat bodies. They claim to know God, and they use the Scriptures. But they are like the Pharisees, blind guides who speak only half-truths. Your only defense against such groups is a strong, personal acquaintance with God's Word. Study for yourself. Consult with reliable pastors of fundamental churches who can show you God's message from the Bible.

Become a reader, especially of the Bible. It is your lifeline!

A Subtle Danger

In the heart of each Christian lies the desire to be all God wants him to be. There is an intensity, a yearning, to be more like Jesus in all of His magnificent fullness. This is natural, and it is to be commended.

But just as any good thing carried to excess becomes a bad thing, so it is with an unbalanced devotion to personal holiness. I have personally known people to devote so much time to prayer and Bible study (between eight and twelve hours daily) that they had no time for people or the church! This is *not* healthy; neither is it true spirituality. Still, there is the burden to be more than we are. What should we do?

In the record of Church history we see various ones who sought to lay hold of God. They fasted, prayed, studied the Word of God and wrestled with demons most of the day and night. Soon these individuals found it necessary to get away from society-at-large so that they might be even less distracted from their spiritual pursuits. The ambition of these persons seemed holy enough, at least on the surface. They practiced self-denial, as our Lord instructed us, with a matchless zeal. Eventually these men came to be highly esteemed for their practices of self-abasement and devotion to God. But how did these persons honor Christ? Where is the proof that they were truly practicing the kind of holy living that God authorizes?

One particular mystic became exceptionally popular with the people for his unmatched devotion. He climbed atop a tall pillar, loaded himself with chains, and spent the next thirty years presumably worshiping God "in pure holiness." The attraction that this man brought to the common people was unbelievable. Even high officials were so impressed by this man's sincerity that they would crouch at the base of his pillar, hoping to catch his excrement. Now this is, to put it plainly, stupid. Still, the people believed that this devoted being was fulfilling God's demands with an exacting degree of excellence. Was he really obeying God? Certainly not!

It is built into us to say we are not perfect. That's good, but it isn't difficult to add to this statement words like these: "I can't be what God expects and have to do such-and-such too"; "I am going to get away and be alone with God"; "If I were a pastor, with nothing to do but read the Bible and pray, I'd be more holy." And on it goes. We excuse ourselves by saying that holiness is not possible unless we become mystical.

The sad fact is that sometimes our self-imposed self-abasement and self-made cry for holiness is Satan's foothold for an attack. "Do you mean to say that by overexerting ourselves in a fleshly attempt to be holy before God that we can actually encounter Satan instead?" Yes.

Paul chided the Colossians by stating, *"Why . . . do you submit to [the world's] rules: 'Do not handle! Do not taste! Do not touch!'? These are all destined to perish with use, because they are based on human commands and teachings. Such regulations indeed have an appearance of wisdom, with their self-imposed worship, their false humility and their harsh treatment of the body, but they lack any value"* (Col. 2:20-23)!

It is possible to seek God, out of a wrong spirit, and actually be faced with satanic responses. Remember the children of Israel. They enjoyed God's blessings, but they wanted more. The "more" led them into God's chastisement. They should have been content.

There are people, Christian people, today who say that they are useless to God unless they get to sing regularly. And they won't be content unless they get to perform in His name. Others say they can't feel God's presence as they used to be able to do. So they will not do anything unless that same sensation returns. Still others state they just have to have more of God; all they want is to be closer, much, much closer to Him.

All of this may sound good—and in some cases it is—but far too often it is simply an escape from the duties God has assigned. Let us learn this truth now: if we cannot find God and serve Him where we are, then we can be certain that moving to some other place in our life will bring us no closer to Him (provided, of course, that our present site is not a sinful one). The notion that the grass is always more holy somewhere else is a trick of Satan.

One of our greatest needs in this hour is to rest contentedly where God has placed us. This exhortation does not, in any degree, imply that we should cease praying or fasting or diligently searching the Scriptures—God forbid! But I am saying that if we are discontented where we find ourselves, then we had better find out what it is about ourselves that needs altering, because God is quite capable of using us—whether we be housewives, cooks, truck drivers, garbage men, salesmen, bankers, secretaries, pastors, or whatever—right where we are now!

Paul writes, *"I have learned to be content whatever the circumstances"* (Phil. 4:11)! This is a truth we, too, must learn if we are to make any sense out of the kind of holiness that pleases God. It isn't mystical encounters or angelic apparitions that make us right with our Lord. These are fine; and blessed are those who receive these rare experiences, but you shouldn't plan on waiting to receive some experience like this before you become holy or it will never happen. You and I can be all God wants right where we are. We don't have to become the president of some religious group or sing solos or even be noticed by anybody. What we need to be used of God is *contentment*—the same thing Paul had!

Look around you. There is the world God has for you. Rejoice in it. Turn this arena into a sanctuary of worship and praise. This is the way all the true saints have had to face life—realistically. God is supernatural and He often displays himself in this manner. But His miracles do not change your world; they are meant to change you so that you can enter your everyday routine with a joy and a peace that wins a broken world to Christ. Leave the mountaintop and go down into the valley. This is where the people are located. And it is where Christ can be found too.

Get involved in your own little world, no matter how insignificant it may appear to the eye, and you will find yourself becoming the kind of person who both pleases God and bears genuine spiritual fruit that will remain long after your years spent on this earth!

Bestselling Books Available at Your Bookseller or use Convenient Tear-Out Order Form
— Quality soft-cover books —

_____ **Ask Me, Lord, I Want to Say Yes**— $1.95
Rosalind Rinker—author of Prayer—
Conversing With God

_____ **Bible and the Bermuda Triangle**— 2.50
Don Tanner and George Johnson
(over 350,000 sold)

_____ **Big Three Mountain-Movers**— 1.95
Jim Bakker—host of PTL-TV

_____ **Challenging Counterfeit**—Raphael Gasson 1.95
Exposé on spiritualism

_____ **Child of Satan—Child of God**— 2.25
Susan Atkins with Bob Slosser
Charles Manson's woman meets God in prison

_____ **Daughter of Destiny**—Kathryn Kuhlman— 1.95
Jamie Buckingham—the most famous woman
preacher—her life—her story

_____ **China: A New Day**—Stanley Mooneyham, 2.50
President of World Vision, gives inside
information and how China fits into your future

_____ **Day the Dollar Dies**—Willard Cantelon 1.95
Your money's future—what to do to protect it

_____ **Do Yourself a Favor: Love Your Wife** 1.95
H. Page Williams (300,000 sold)—the best book
on husband and wife relationships

_____ **How to Flip Your Flab—Forever**—
Harold Hill 2.95
The final-diet book

_____ **Healing Light**—Agnes Sanford 1.95
Over thirty-six printings

Total this side $ _____

(more on other side)

Ask your bookseller for these other bestsellers (or use this convenient tear-out order form)

_____ **Thanks Lord, I Needed That!**—Charlene $2.95
Potterbaum—a housewife's practical view on life
(national bestseller)

_____ **Prison to Praise**—Merlin Carothers   2.50
(over 2 million sold)

_____ **Blueprint for Raising a Child**—Mike   3.95
Phillips—every parent's book

_____ **Worth of a Woman**—Iverna Tompkins   2.95
Teaches women their real worth

_____ **Clap Your Hands!**—Larry Tomczak   2.95
A young Catholic finds his faith

_____ **Total Preparation for Childbirth**—Cher   3.95
Randall—acknowledged as a must for future parents

_____ **Victory on Praise Mountain**—NEW!   2.95
Merlin Carothers—the best since Prison to Praise

_____ **Closer Than My Shadow**—Diane Hanny   3.95
A Christian meditation for youth

_____ **People's Temple—People's Tomb**—   2.25
Phil Kerns and Doug Wead
The real story of Jim Jones' cult—
A national bestseller made into a movie

_____ **Holy Spirit and You**—Dennis and Rita   3.50
Bennett   The bestselling book on the
charismatic experience—over 300,000 sold

Total $_____

If unavailable at local bookstores, order through:
LIF BOOKS — Box 191, Plainfield, NJ 07061

Please enclose payment—Sorry, no C.O.D.s—Add 50¢ for
first book, 35¢ for each additional book for postage and
handling

Name _____

Address _____

City _____State _____ZIP _____